Macmillan McGraw-Hill

W9-DJD-715

Math Connects

2

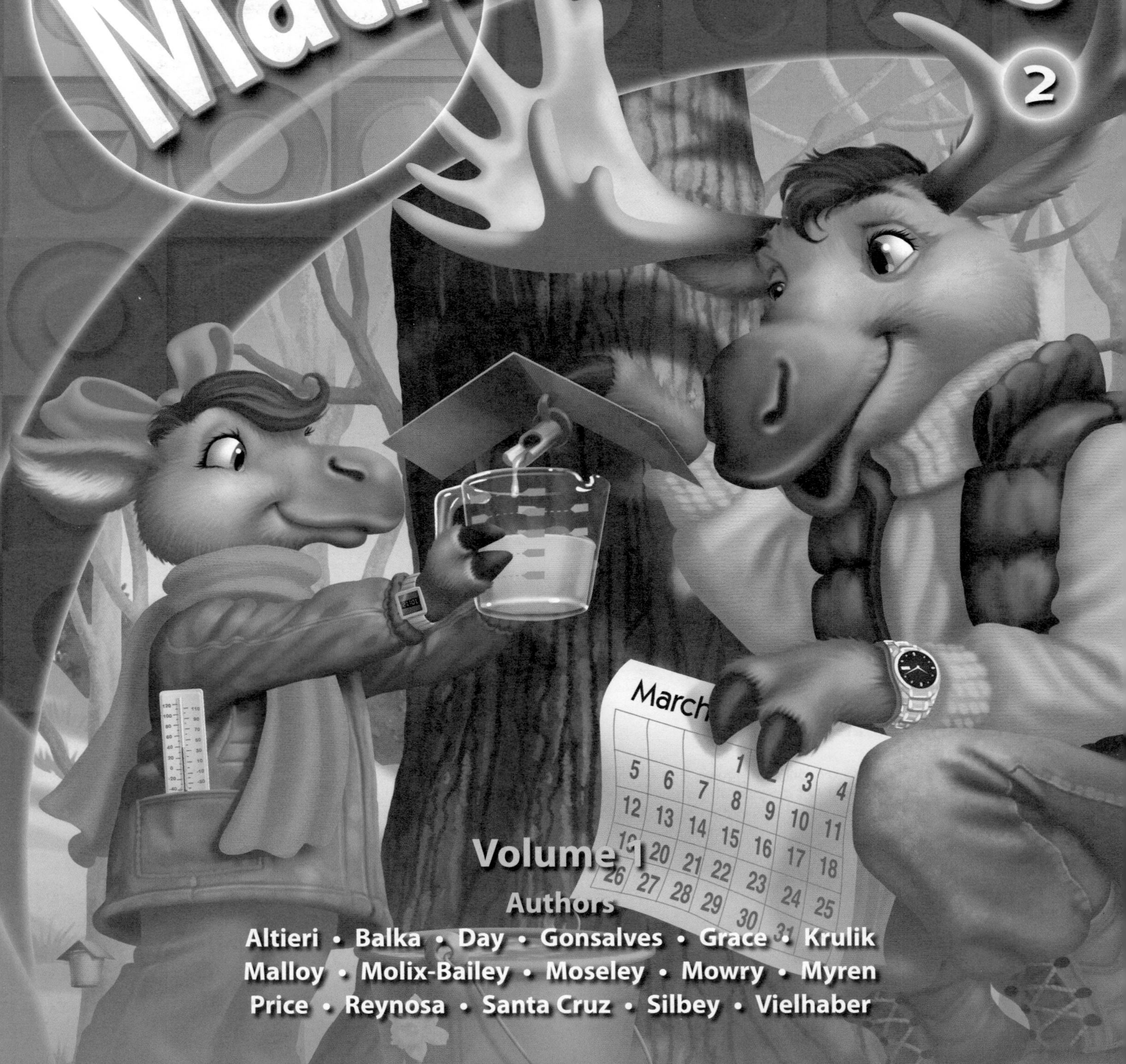

Volume 1

Authors

Altieri • Balka • Day • Gonsalves • Grace • Krulik
Malloy • Molix-Bailey • Moseley • Mowry • Myren
Price • Reynosa • Santa Cruz • Silbey • Vielhaber

Mc
Graw
Hill
Macmillan/McGraw-Hill

T60383

About the Cover

Measurement is a featured topic in Second grade. On the cover, the moose is measuring the amount of sap coming out of the maple tree. What other measurements can students find on the cover?

The McGraw-Hill Companies

 Macmillan/McGraw-Hill

Send all inquiries to:
Macmillan/McGraw-Hill
8787 Orion Place
Columbus, OH 43240-4027

Volume 1
ISBN: 978-0-02-105727-6
MHID: 0-02-105727-3

Math Connects, Grade 2

Printed in the United States of America.

7 8 9 10 RJE/LEH 16 15 14 13 12 11 10

Contents in Brief

Focal Points and Connections
See page iv for key.

Start Smart

Looking Ahead

Problem-Solving Projects

The Curriculum Focal Points identify key mathematical ideas for this grade. They are not discrete topics or a checklist to be mastered; rather, they provide a framework for the majority of instruction at a particular grade level and the foundation for future mathematics study. The complete document may be viewed at www.nctm.org/focalpoints.

G2-FP1   *Number and Operations:* **Developing an understanding of the base-ten numeration system and place-value concepts**

Children develop an understanding of the base-ten numeration system and place-value concepts (at least to 1000). Their understanding of base-ten numeration includes ideas of counting in units and multiples of hundreds, tens, and ones, as well as a grasp of number relationships, which they demonstrate in a variety of ways, including comparing and ordering numbers. They understand multidigit numbers in terms of place value, recognizing that place-value notation is a shorthand for the sums of multiples of powers of 10 (e.g., 853 as 8 hundreds + 5 tens + 3 ones).

G2-FP2   *Number and Operations* and *Algebra:* **Developing quick recall of addition facts and related subtraction facts and fluency with multidigit addition and subtraction**

Children use their understanding of addition to develop quick recall of basic addition facts and related subtraction facts. They solve arithmetic problems by applying their understanding of models of addition and subtraction (such as combining or separating sets or using number lines), relationships and properties of number (such as place value), and properties of addition (commutativity and associativity). Children develop, discuss, and use efficient, accurate, and generalizable methods to add and subtract multidigit whole numbers. They select and apply appropriate methods to estimate sums and differences or calculate them mentally, depending on the context and numbers involved. They develop fluency with efficient procedures, including standard algorithms, for adding and subtracting whole numbers, understand why the procedures work (on the basis of place value and properties of operations), and use them to solve problems.

G2-FP3   *Measurement:* **Developing an understanding of linear measurement and facility in measuring lengths**

Children develop an understanding of the meaning and processes of measurement, including such underlying concepts as partitioning (the mental activity of slicing the length of an object into equal-sized units) and transitivity (e.g., if object A is longer than object B and object B is longer than object C, then object A is longer than object C). They understand linear measure as an iteration of units and use rulers and other measurement tools with that understanding. They understand the need for equal-length units, the use of standard units of measure (centimeter and inch), and the inverse relationship between the size of a unit and the number of units used in a particular measurement (i.e., children recognize that the smaller the unit, the more iterations they need to cover a given length).

G2-FP4C *Number and Operations:* Children use place value and properties of operations to create equivalent representations of given numbers (such as 35 represented by 35 ones, 3 tens and 5 ones, or 2 tens and 15 ones) and to write, compare, and order multidigit numbers. They use these ideas to compose and decompose multidigit numbers. Children add and subtract to solve a variety of problems, including applications involving measurement, geometry, and data, as well as nonroutine problems. In preparation for grade 3, they solve problems involving multiplicative situations, developing initial understandings of multiplication as repeated addition.

G2-FP5C *Geometry* and *Measurement:* Children estimate, measure, and compute lengths as they solve problems involving data, space, and movement through space. By composing and decomposing two-dimensional shapes (intentionally substituting arrangements of smaller shapes for larger shapes or substituting larger shapes for many smaller shapes), they use geometric knowledge and spatial reasoning to develop foundations for understanding area, fractions, and proportions.

G2-FP6C *Algebra:* Children use number patterns to extend their knowledge of properties of numbers and operations. For example, when skip counting, they build foundations for understanding multiples and factors

Authors

Mary Behr Altieri
Putnam/Northern
   Westchester BOCES
Yorktown Heights,
   New York

Don S. Balka
Professor Emeritus
Saint Mary's College
Notre Dame, Indiana

Roger Day, Ph.D.
Mathematics Department Chair
Pontiac Township High School
Pontiac, Illinois

Philip D. Gonsalves
Mathematics Coordinator
Alameda County Office
   of Education and
   California State
   University East Bay
Hayward, California

Ellen C. Grace
Consultant
Albuquerque,
   New Mexico

Stephen Krulik
Professor Emeritus
   Mathematics Education
Temple University
Cherry Hill, New Jersey

Carol E. Malloy, Ph.D.
Associate Professor of
   Mathematics Education
University of North
   Carolina at Chapel Hill
Chapel Hill, North
   Carolina

Rhonda J. Molix-Bailey
Mathematics Consultant
Mathematics by Design
Desoto, Texas

Lois Gordon Moseley
Staff Developer
NUMBERS: Mathematics
   Professional
   Development
Houston, Texas

Brian Mowry
Independent Math Educational
   Consultant/Part-Time Pre-K
   Instructional Specialist
Austin Independent School District
Austin, Texas

Math Online > Meet the Authors at macmillanmh.com

Christina L. Myren
Consultant Teacher
Conejo Valley Unified
    School District
Thousand Oaks, California

Jack Price
Professor Emeritus
California State
    Polytechnic University
Pomona, California

Mary Esther Reynosa
Instructional Specialist for
    Elementary Mathematics
Northside Independent
    School District
San Antonio, Texas

Rafaela M. Santa Cruz
SDSU/CGU Doctoral
    Program in Education
San Diego State University
San Diego, California

Robyn Silbey
Math Content Coach
Montgomery County
    Public Schools
Gaithersburg, Maryland

Kathleen Vielhaber
Mathematics Consultant
St. Louis, Missouri

Contributing Authors

Donna J. Long
Mathematics Consultant
Indianapolis, Indiana

FOLDABLES **Dinah Zike**
Educational Consultant
Dinah-Might Activities, Inc.
San Antonio, Texas

Consultants

Macmillan/McGraw-Hill wishes to thank the following professionals for their feedback. They were instrumental in providing valuable input toward the development of this program in these specific areas.

Mathematical Content

Viken Hovsepian
Professor of Mathematics
Rio Hondo College
Whittier, California

Grant A. Fraser, Ph.D.
Professor of Mathematics
California State University, Los Angeles
Los Angeles, California

Arthur K. Wayman, Ph.D.
Professor of Mathematics Emeritus
California State University, Long Beach
Long Beach, California

Assessment

Jane D. Gawronski, Ph.D.
Director of Assessment and Outreach
San Diego State University
San Diego, California

Cognitive Guided Instruction

Susan B. Empson, Ph.D.
Associate Professor of Mathematics
   and Science Education
University of Texas at Austin
Austin, Texas

English Learners

Cheryl Avalos
Mathematics Consultant
Los Angeles County Office of Education, Retired
Hacienda Heights, California

Kathryn Heinze
Graduate School of Education
Hamline University
St. Paul, Minnesota

Family Involvement

Paul Giganti, Jr.
Mathematics Education Consultant
Albany, California

Literature

David M. Schwartz
Children's Author, Speaker, Storyteller
Oakland, California

Vertical Alignment

Berchie Holliday
National Educational Consultant
Silver Spring, Maryland

Deborah A. Hutchens, Ed.D.
Principal
Norfolk Highlands Elementary
Chesapeake, Virginia

Reviewers

Each Reviewer reviewed at least two chapters of the Student Edition, giving feedback and suggestions for improving the effectiveness of the mathematics instruction.

Ernestine D. Austin
Facilitating Teacher/Basic Skills Teacher
LORE School
Ewing, NJ

Susie Bellah
Kindergarten Teacher
Lakeland Elementary
Humble, TX

Megan Bennett
Elementary Math Coordinator
Hartford Public Schools
Hartford, CT

Susan T. Blankenship
5th Grade Teacher – Math
Stanford Elementary School
Stanford, KY

Wendy Buchanan
3rd Grade Teacher
The Classical Center at Vial
Garland, TX

Sandra Signorelli Coelho
Associate Director for Mathematics
PIMMS at Wesleyan University
Middletown, CT

Joanne DeMizio
Asst. Supt., Math and Science Curriculum
Archdiocese of New York
New York, NY

Anthony Dentino
Supervisor of Mathematics
Brick Township Schools
Brick, NJ

Lorrie L. Drennon
Math Teacher
Collins Middle School
Corsicana, TX

Ethel A. Edwards
Director of Curriculum and Instruction
Topeka Public Schools
Topeka, KS

Carolyn Elender
District Elementary Math Instructional Specialist
Pasadena ISD
Pasadena, TX

Monica Engel
Educator Second Grade
Pioneer Elementary School
Bolingbrook, IL

Anna Dahinden Flynn
Math Teacher
Coulson Tough K–6 Elementary
The Woodlands, TX

Brenda M. Foxx
Principal
University Park Elementary
University Park, MD

Katherine A. Frontier
Elementary Teacher
Laidlaw
Western Springs, IL

Susan J. Furphy
5th Grade Teacher
Nisley Elementary
Grand Junction, CO

Peter Gatz
Student Services Coordinator
Brooks Elementary
Aurora, IL

Amber Gregersen
Teacher – 2nd Grade
Nisley Elementary
Grand Junction, CO

Roberta Grindle
Math and Language Arts Academic Intervention
    Service Provider
Cumberland Head Elementary School
Plattsburgh, NY

Sr. Helen Lucille Habig, RSM
Assistant Superintendent/Mathematics
Archdiocese of Cincinnati
Cincinnati, OH

Holly L. Hepp
Math Facilitator
Barringer Academic Center
Charlotte, NC

Martha J. Hickman
2nd Grade Teacher
Dr. James Craik Elementary School
Pomfret, MD

Margie Hill
District Coordinating Teacher for Mathematics,
    K–12
Blue Valley USD 229
Overland Park, KS

Carol H. Joyce
5th Grade Teacher
Nathanael Greene Elementary
Liberty, NC

Stella K. Kostante
Curriculum Coach
Roosevelt Elementary
Pittsburgh, PA

Pamela Fleming Lowe
Fourth Grade eMINTS Teacher
O'Neal Elementary
Poplar Bluff, MO

Lauren May, NBCT
4th Grade Teacher
May Watts Elementary School
Naperville, IL

Lorraine Moore
Grade 3 Math Teacher
Cowpens Elementary School
Cowpens, SC

Shannon L. Moorhead
4th Grade Teacher
Centerville Elementary
Anderson, SC

Gina M. Musselman, M.Ed
Kindergarten Teacher
Padeo Verde Elementary
Peoria, AZ

Jen Neufeld
3rd Grade Teacher
Kendall
Naperville, IL

Cathie Osiecki
K–5 Mathematics Coordinator
Middletown Public Schools
Middletown, CT

Phyllis L. Pacilli
Elementary Education Teacher
Fullerton Elementary
Addison, IL

Cindy Pearson
4th/5th Grade Teacher
John D. Spicer Elementary
Haltom City, TX

Herminio M. Planas
Mathematics Curriculum Specialist
Administrative Offices-Bridgeport Public Schools
Bridgeport, CT

Jo J. Puree
Educator
Lackamas Elementary
Yelm, WA

Teresa M. Reynolds
Third Grade Teacher
Forrest View Elementary
Everett, WA

Dr. John A. Rhodes
Director of Mathematics
Indian Prairie SD #204
Aurora, IL

Amy Romm
1st Grade Teacher
Starline Elementary
Lake Havasu, AZ

Delores M. Rushing
Numeracy Coach
Dept. of Academic Services-Mathematics
    Department
Washington, DC

Daniel L. Scudder
Mathematics/Technology Specialist
Boone Elementary
Houston, TX

Laura Seymour
Resource Teacher Leader – Elementary Math &
    Science, Retired
Dearborn Public Schools
Dearborn, MI

Petra Siprian
Teacher
Army Trail Elementary School
Addison, IL

Sandra Stein
K-5 Mathematics Consultant
St. Clair County Regional Educational Service Agency
Marysville, MI

Barb Stoflet
Curriculum Specialist
Roseville Area Schools
Roseville, MN

Kim Summers
Principal
Dynard Elementary
Chaptico, MD

Ann C. Teater
4th Grade Teacher
Lancaster Elementary
Lancaster, KY

Anne E. Tunney
Teacher
City of Erie School District
Erie, PA

Joylien Weathers
1st Grade Teacher
Mesa View Elementary
Grand Junction, CO

Christine F. Weiss
Third Grade Teacher
Robert C. Hill Elementary School
Romeoville, IL

Contents

Start Smart

CHAPTER 1

Use Place Value to 100 and Patterns

= Hands-On Activity

= Technology Link

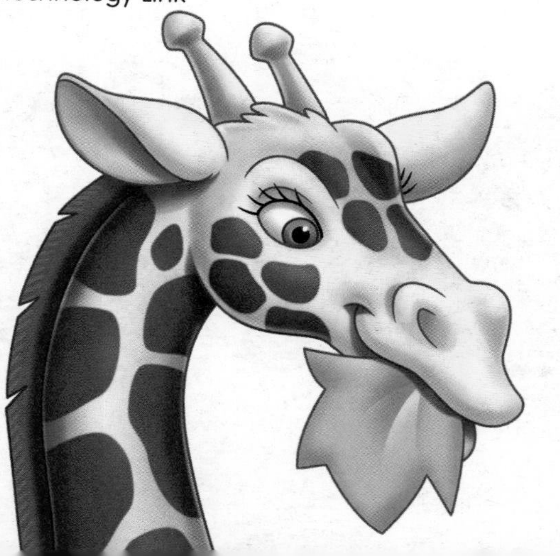

Focal Points and Connections
See page iv for key.

G2-FP1 *Number and Operations*
G2-FP6C *Algebra*

H.O.T. Problems
Higher Order Thinking 28, 30

Problem Solving 20, 36, 40, 44

WRITING IN MATH 24

Contents

Focal Points and Connections
See page iv for key.

G2-FP2 *Number and Operations* and *Algebra*

H.O.T. Problems
Higher Order Thinking 56, 72

Problem Solving 64, 68

WRITING IN ▶MATH 60

Contents

CHAPTER 3 Apply Subtraction Concepts

 = Hands-On Activity

Focal Points and Connections
See page iv for key.

G2-FP2 *Number and Operations* and *Algebra*

H.O.T. Problems
   Higher Order Thinking 90, 102, 104

Problem Solving 98

WRITING IN ▶ MATH 88

Contents

Focal Points and Connections
See page iv for key.

G2-FP4C *Number and Operations*

H.O.T. Problems
Higher Order Thinking 122

Problem Solving 118, 120, 134

Writing in Math 128

Contents

 = Hands-On Activity

Focal Points and Connections
See page iv for key.

G2-FP2 *Number and Operations* and *Algebra*

H.O.T. Problems
Higher Order Thinking 158

Problem Solving 148, 150, 160, 164

WRITING IN MATH 154

Contents

Focal Points and Connections
See page iv for key.

G2-FP2 *Number and Operations* and *Algebra*

H.O.T. Problems
Higher Order Thinking 182, 200

Problem Solving 180, 190, 192

WRITING IN ▸MATH 184

CHAPTER 7
Determine the Value of Money

= Hands-On Activity

= Technology Link

Focal Points and Connections
See page iv for key.

G2-FP4C *Number and Operations*
G2-FP6C *Algebra*

H.O.T. Problems
Higher Order Thinking 216

Problem Solving 214, 218, 230, 232

Contents

**Focal Points
and Connections**
See page iv for key.

G2-FP3 *Measurement*
G2-FP5C *Geometry* and *Measurement*

H.O.T. Problems
   Higher Order Thinking 260

Problem Solving 248, 262, 270

WRITING IN MATH 252

Contents

= Hands-On Activity

Focal Points and Connections
See page iv for key.

G2-FP5C *Geometry* and *Measurement*

H.O.T. Problems
Higher Order Thinking 286, 294

Problem Solving 290, 298

WRITING IN MATH 284

Contents

Focal Points and Connections
See page iv for key.

G2-FP1 *Number and Operations*
G2-FP4C *Number and Operations*

H.O.T. Problems
Higher Order Thinking 320, 332

Problem Solving 324, 330, 334

WRITING IN MATH 314

Contents

= Hands-On Activity

Focal Points and Connections
See page iv for key.

G2-FP5C *Geometry* and *Measurement*

H.O.T. Problems
Higher Order Thinking 348, 366

Problem Solving 346, 358, 360, 362

WRITING IN ▶MATH 368

Contents

Focal Points and Connections
See page iv for key.

G2-FP3 *Measurement*
G2-FP5C *Geometry* and *Measurement*

H.O.T. Problems
Higher Order Thinking 394

Problem Solving 382, 392, 396

WRITING IN ►MATH 388

Contents

= Hands-On Activity

Focal Points and Connections
See page iv for key.

G2-FP3 *Measurement*
G2-FP5C *Geometry* and *Measurement*

H.O.T. Problems
Higher Order Thinking 418, 426

Problem Solving 410, 422

WRITING IN ►MATH 412

Contents

Focal Points and Connections
See page iv for key.

G2-FP2 *Number and Operations* and *Algebra*

H.O.T. Problems
Higher Order Thinking 442, 452, 454

Problem Solving 440, 458

WRITING IN ▶MATH 448, 460

Contents

= Hands-On Activity

Focal Points and Connections
See page iv for key.

G2-FP4C *Number and Operations*
G2-FP6C *Algebra*

H.O.T. Problems
Higher Order Thinking 490

Problem Solving 476, 480

WRITING IN ▸MATH 474, 488

XXV

Contents

Looking Ahead

H.O.T. Problems
Higher Order Thinking LA6, LA14

Problem Solving LA4, LA10

WRITING IN ►MATH LA8, LA12

Problem-Solving Projects

Contents

Student Handbook

Start Smart

Let's Review!

Bald Eagle

Name: _____

Sea Shells in South Carolina

South Carolina has 187 miles of coastline along the Atlantic Ocean.

Porter found 5 shells. Sophia found 3.
How many shells did they find in all?

Understand

What do I know? Underline what you know.
What do I need to find? Circle the question.

Did you Know?

Scientists study shell mounds on the beaches of South Carolina to learn about the state's history.

Plan

How will I solve the problem?

Solve

Write a number sentence.

_____ + _____ = _____ shells

Check

Look back.
Is my answer reasonable?

Name: _____

Berries in North Carolina

Strawberries and blueberries are the state berries of North Carolina.

Add. Then write the number word.

1.

   5 + 4 = _____   _____

2.

   2 + 3 = _____   _____

3.

   6 + 1 = _____   _____

Copyright © Macmillan/McGraw-Hill, a division of The McGraw-Hill Companies, Inc.

Did you Know?

Many people go to the North Carolina Strawberry Festival in Chadbourn each May.

Subtract. Then write the number word.

4.  8 − 2 = _____ _____

5.  9 − 6 = _____ _____

6.  7 − 5 = _____ _____

7. **WRITING IN ►MATH** Look at the picture. Write a number story. Ask a friend to solve the problem.

_____

_____

_____

_____

_____

Name: _____

Horses in Kentucky

Kentucky is famous for its prize-winning horses.

Use the picture to solve.

1. How many horses are in the picture above?

    _____ horses

2. Two more horses join them. How many horses are there now?

    _____ horses

3. Write a number sentence to show how many horses there are in all.

    _____ + _____ = _____ horses

Did you Know?

The Kentucky Derby is the oldest ongoing horse race in the country.

Write a number sentence to solve.

4. Five horses are in a barn. Four more horses arrive.
How many horses are in the barn now?

_____ + _____ = _____ horses

5. Nine horses are in a barn. Five of the horses leave.
How many horses are left in the barn?

_____ − _____ = _____ horses

6. There are 4 black horses and 5 brown horses.
How many horses are there altogether?

_____ + _____ = _____ horses

7. WRITING IN ▸MATH Use the picture to write a number
problem. Ask a friend to solve the problem.

_____

_____

_____

Start Smart

Name: _____

4 Measurement

Monuments in New York

The Statue of Liberty in New York City is a symbol of freedom.

Look at the picture to solve.

1. About how many small ⊂▭⊃ tall is the picture of the Statue of Liberty?

   about _____ ⊂▭⊃ tall

2. Find something in your classroom that is about 3 small ⊂▭⊃ long. What did you find?

   _____

Look at the picture to solve.

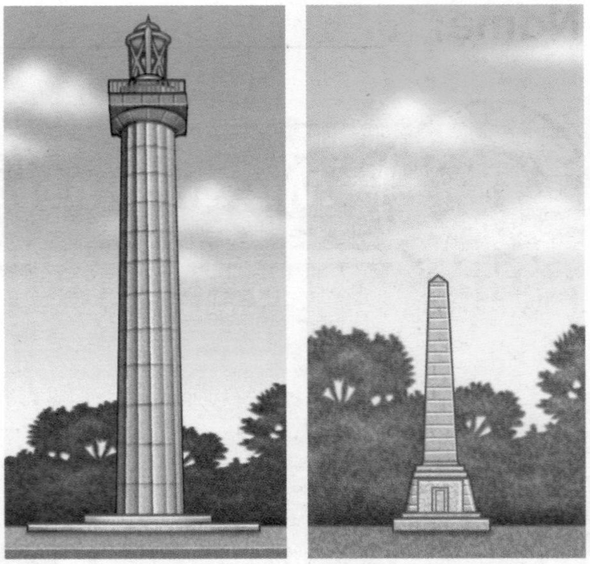

3. Use a small ⬭ to measure
the height of each monument.

Monument 1:

about _____ small ⬭ tall

Monument 2:

about _____ small ⬭ tall

Monument 1   Monument 2

4. Compare your measurements from
Exercise 3. What did you find?

_____

_____

_____

5. **WRITING IN ►MATH** Use a straw to measure an object in
the classroom. Use a small paper clip to measure the same
object. What difference did you see? Explain your answer.

_____

_____

_____

_____

Name: _____

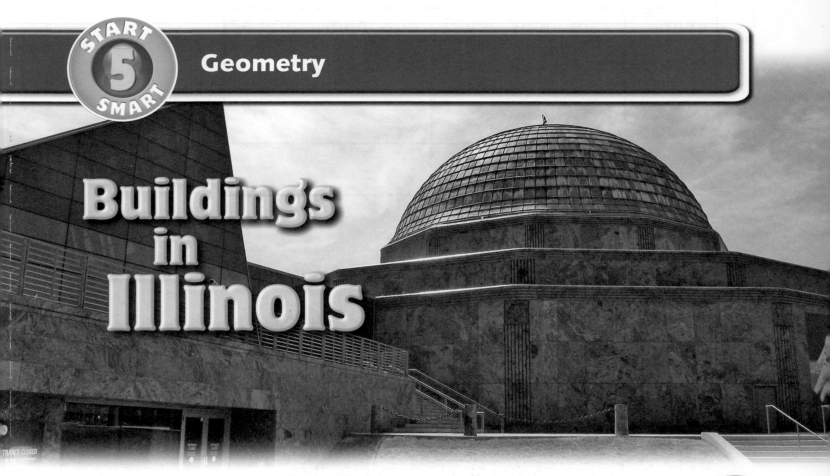

Buildings in Illinois

The Adler Planetarium in Chicago, Illinois, is the oldest planetarium in use today.

1. Draw a line to match the figures.

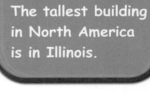

2. How many sides and corners does each figure have?

Figure	How many sides?	How many corners?

3. Compare the figures. Circle the figures that are flat.

4. |WRITING IN ►MATH Think of all the figures you know.
Use as many figures as you can to draw a picture
of a building in the space below.

Which figures did you use?

_____

Name: _____

Amusement Parks in Ohio

Did you Know?

There are about 50 thousand feet of roller coaster track at Cedar Point, an amusement park in Sandusky, Ohio.

Some of the world's tallest and fastest roller coasters can be found in Ohio.

Look at the picture graph. It shows how many boys and girls visited the amusement park today. Use the picture graph to answer the questions.

Visitors to the Amusement Park								
Boys	🧑	🧑	🧑	🧑	🧑	🧑		
Girls	👧	👧	👧	👧	👧	👧	👧	👧

1. How many children visited the amusement park? _____

2. How many girls visited the amusement park? _____

3. Did more boys or girls visit the amusement park? _____

Use the bar graph to answer the questions.

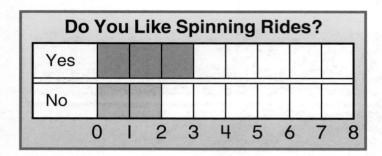

Do You Like Spinning Rides?

4. How many children like spinning rides? _____

5. How many children took this survey? _____

Ask 5 classmates if they like roller coasters. Use your
results to fill in the bar graph and answer the questions.

Do You Like Roller Coasters?

6. How many classmates do not like roller coasters? _____

7. Which group do you think would like to visit an
amusement park? Tell how you know.

_____

_____

8. **WRITING IN ►MATH** Write a sentence that tells
about your bar graph.

_____

_____

CHAPTER 1

Use Place Value to 100 and Patterns

▶ **Key Vocabulary**

- ones
- tens
- estimate
- compare
- pattern

Explore

This caterpillar has a pattern on its body. Can you see it? Draw the pattern.

Name _____

Are You Ready for Chapter 1?

Write the number of each. Circle the group that has more.

1.

_____ trucks   _____ cars

Match the number word and the number.

2. ten   8

3. three   10

4. eight   3

Write the missing numbers.

5.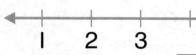

 1   2   3   __   5   __   __   8   __   10

Write the numbers in order from least to greatest.

6. 2, 9, 4, 3   _____, _____, _____, _____

7. Ben found these 4 note cards on the sidewalk.

| five | six | one | seven |
| 5 | 6 | 1 | 7 |

Help Ben put the note cards in order.

[ ] [ ] [ ] [ ]

This page checks skills needed for Chapter 1.

Dear Family,

Today my class started Chapter 1, **Use Place Value to 100 and Patterns**. In this chapter, I will learn to estimate, compare, and order numbers through 100. Here is an activity we can do and a list of books we can read together.

Love,

_____

Activity

Pour some raisins onto a plate. Have your child estimate the number of raisins. Then count to find how close the estimate is. Continue to change the amount and estimate. See if your child's estimates get closer to the actual number.

Key Vocabulary

place value the value given to a digit by its place in a number

estimate to find a number close to an exact amount

Math Online ▷ Click on the eGlossary link at macmillanmh.com to find out more about these words. There are 13 languages.

Books to Read

Spunky Monkeys on Parade
by Stuart J. Murphy
HarperCollins
Publishing, 1999.

More or Less
by Stuart J. Murphy
HarperTrophy
Publishing, 2005.

The Father Who Had 10 Children
by Benedicte Guettier
Penguin Young Readers
Group, 2001.

Estimada familia:

Hoy mi clase comenzó el Capítulo 1, **Usa el valor de posición hasta 100 y patrones**. En este capítulo, aprenderé a estimar, a comparar y a ordenar números hasta 100. A continuación, hay una actividad que podemos hacer y una lista de libros que podemos leer juntos.

Cariños, _____

Actividad

Viertan sobre un plato algunas pasitas. Pídanle a su hijo(a) que estime el número de pasitas y que luego las cuente para averiguar la certeza de la conjetura. Cambien varias veces la cantidad y estimen. Verifiquen si la conjetura de su hijo(a) se acerca más al número real.

Vocabulario clave

valor de posición valor dado a un dígito de acuerdo con su posición en el número

estimar hallar un número que se acerca a una cantidad exacta

Math Online > Visiten el enlace eGlossary en macmillanmh.com para averiguar más sobre estas palabras, las cuales se muestran en 13 idiomas.

Libros recomendados

Llaman a la puerta
de Pat Hutchins
Live Oak Media, 2005.

El papá que tenía 10 hijos
de Bénédicte Guettier
Puffin, 2001.

Tens and Ones

Get Ready

Main Idea

I will group ones to make ten.

Vocabulary

ones

tens

I can group ones to make tens.

You can group 10 **ones** as 1 **ten**.

10 ones = __1__ ten

70 ones = __7__ tens

90 ones = __9__ tens

You can also group tens and ones.

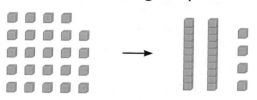

24 is 2 tens and 4 ones.

24 ones = __2__ tens __4__ ones   20 + 4 = __24__

Write how many.

1.

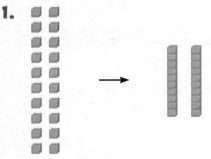

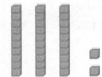 ____20____ ones = ____2____ tens

2.

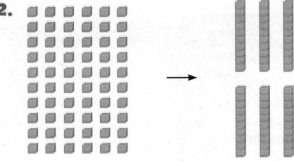

____ ones = ____ tens

Write how many tens and ones. Then write the number.

3.

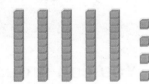

____3____ tens ____2____ ones

____30____ + ____2____ = ____32____

4.

____ tens ____ ones

____ + ____ = ____

5.

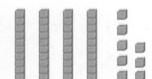

____ tens ____ ones

____ + ____ = ____

6.

____ tens ____ ones

____ + ____ = ____

---

7. **Talk About It** Explain how 26 is different from 62.

GO on

Name _____

Write how many.

8.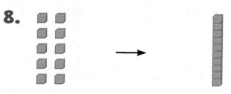

_____ ones = _____ ten

9.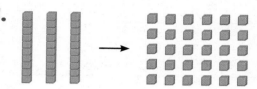

_____ tens = _____ ones

10.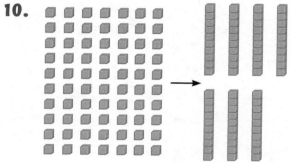

_____ ones = _____ tens

11.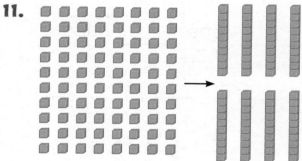

_____ ones = _____ tens

Write how many tens and ones.
Then write the number.

12.

_____ tens _____ ones

_____ + _____ = _____

13.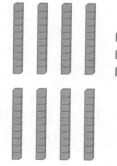

_____ tens _____ ones

_____ + _____ = _____

Write how many tens and ones. Then write the number.

14.

_____ ten _____ one

_____ + _____ = _____

15.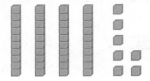

_____ tens _____ ones

_____ + _____ = _____

16.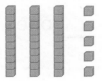

_____ tens _____ ones

_____ + _____ = _____

17.

_____ ten _____ ones

_____ + _____ = _____

18.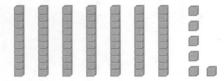

_____ tens _____ ones

_____ + _____ = _____

19.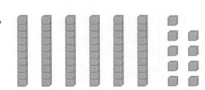

_____ tens _____ ones

_____ + _____ = _____

Problem Solving

20. Number Sense Juan has 4 packs of baseball cards. Each pack has 10 cards. He has 3 more cards in his pocket. How many baseball cards does Juan have?

_____ baseball cards

Math at Home Activity: Write some 2-digit numbers, such as 67, and have your child tell you how many tens and how many ones (6 tens and 7 ones).

Name _____

Place Value to 100

Get Ready

Main Idea

I will find the place value in numbers to 100.

Vocabulary

digit

place value

The place of a **digit** in a number tells its value. The digits in 29 are 2 and 9. What is the **place value** of each digit in 29?

___2___ tens ___9___ ones

2 tens = 20   9 ones = 9

Check

Circle the value of the **red** digit.

1. 25

(5) or 50

2. 34

3   or   30

3. 18

8   or   80

4. 42

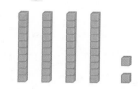

2   or   20

5. Talk About It   Is 3 tens and 9 ones greater than 9 tens and 3 ones? Explain.

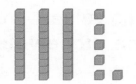
Circle the value of the **red** digit.

6. 36

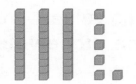

6 or 60

7. 29

2 or 20

8. 33

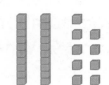

3 or 30

9. 41

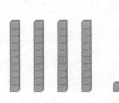

1 or 10

10. 28

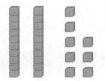

8 or 80

11. 12

1 or 10

12. 39

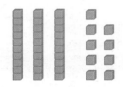

3 or 30

13. 24

4 or 40

14. 65

6 or 60

15. 90

9 or 90

16. 21

1 or 10

17. 47

7 or 70

18. 81

8 or 80

19. 26

6 or 60

20. 39

9 or 90

21. 73

7 or 70

22. 25

2 or 20

23. 53

3 or 30

24. 75

5 or 50

25. 50

5 or 50

Math at Home Activity: Look at a newspaper. Find two-digit numbers. Ask your child to name the tens and ones.

Name _____

 **Practice** with Technology

Click on 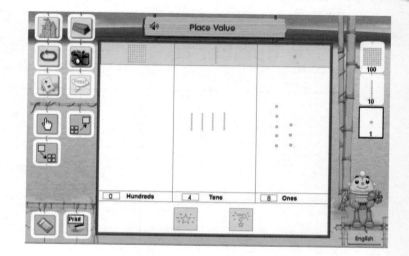 .
Choose Place Value Chart.

Stamp out 4 ▭▭▭▭▭ .

Stamp out 8 ▪ .

What is the number? _48_

26. Use ▦ to stamp tens and ones.
   Then write the number.

Stamp		What is the number?
▯	▪	
2	9	
5	2	
7	9	
8	6	
4	4	
9	8	

Remember, the place of a digit tells its value.

27. Use [image] to stamp the value of the **red** digit. Show your work.

The number is:	Stamp	
	[long bar icon]	[small square icon]
4**9**		
2**4**		
61		
52		
7**8**		

28. **WRITING IN** ►**MATH**

Cindy has 87 pennies. She needs 78 pennies to buy a pen. Does she have enough money? How do you know?

_____

_____

_____

78¢

Name _____

Problem-Solving Strategy
Use Logical Reasoning

Main Idea

I will use logical reasoning to solve problems.

A hamster, a snake, and a frog are kept in 3 cages. The hamster is in the cage that is the same color as a stop sign. The snake is not in the cage that is the same color as the sun. Which animal is in each cage?

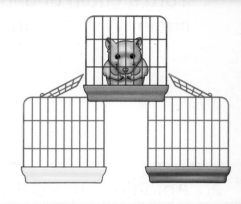

Understand

What do I need to find?
Circle the question.

Plan

How will I solve the problem?

Solve

Use logical reasoning.

Check

Look back.
Is my answer reasonable?

Try It

Use logical reasoning to solve.

Remember
Understand
Plan
Solve
Check

1. Dion's chain is the shortest. Jasmine's chain is shorter than Toru's chain and longer than Dion's chain. Who has the longest chain?

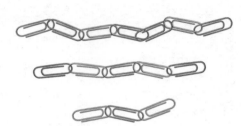

_____ has the longest chain.

---

2. Antonio is more than 7 years old.
   He is less than 10 years old.
   He is not 8 years old.
   How old is Antonio?

Antonio is _____ years old.

Your Turn

Use logical reasoning to solve.

3. Each dinosaur is a different color. From left to right, the green dinosaur is between the red one and brown one. The purple dinosaur is first. The red dinosaur is last. What is the order of the dinosaurs from left to right?

_____, _____, _____, _____

---

4. Elki picked a number. The digit in the tens place is two greater than the digit in the ones place. The sum of these digits is 8. What number did Elki pick?

Elki picked _____.

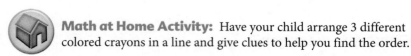

Math at Home Activity: Have your child arrange 3 different colored crayons in a line and give clues to help you find the order.

Read and Write Numbers

 **Get Ready**

Main Idea

I will read and write numbers.

You can write numbers as words. Each number has a name. 16 is sixteen.

Numbers to 20			
1	one	11	eleven
2	two	12	twelve
3	three	13	thirteen
4	four	14	fourteen
5	five	15	fifteen
6	six	16	sixteen
7	seven	17	seventeen
8	eight	18	eighteen
9	nine	19	nineteen
10	ten	20	twenty

Tens	
10	ten
20	twenty
30	thirty
40	forty
50	fifty
60	sixty
70	seventy
80	eighty
90	ninety
100	one hundred

 Check

Write each number.

1. thirty-five   35

2. seventy _____

3. sixty-three _____

4. forty-one _____

Write each number name.

5. 14 _____

6. 80 _____

7. **Talk About It**   How do you know what digits to use to write twenty-three?

Write each number or number name.

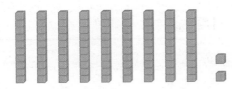

8. eleven

_____

9. seventy-two

_____

10. thirty-six

_____

11. eighty

_____

12. seven

_____

13. sixty-eight

_____

14. twenty-seven

_____

15. fourteen

_____

16. eighty-six

_____

17. one hundred

_____

18. thirteen

_____

19. forty-three

_____

20. ninety

_____

21. twenty-two

_____

22. fifty-eight

_____

23. seventy-seven

_____

24. ninety-four

_____

25. sixty-one

_____

26. 15

_____

27. 70

_____

28. 40

_____

H.O.T. Problem

29. Thinking Math What are two ways to write this number?

_____

_____

Math at Home Activity: Write a 2-digit number, such as 17. Ask your child to write and read the number name.

Estimate Amounts

Get Ready

Main Idea

I will estimate to find about how many.

Vocabulary

estimate

Sometimes you do not need an exact number. An **estimate** tells *about* how many there are.

?   **10 marbles**

First: Look at the group of ten.

Next: Compare it to the unknown number.

Last: Write your estimate.

about _30_ marbles

It looks like about 3 groups of ten or 30 marbles.

Check

Estimate about how many. Circle the answer.

1.

?   **10 buttons**

| about 30 | about 60 | about 90 |

2.

?   **10 strawberries**

| about 20 | about 40 | about 80 |

3. **Talk About It** Explain how you estimated.

Estimate about how many. Circle the answer.

4.

? 　　　　　**10 pencils**

about　　　about　　　about
20　　　　　40　　　　　90

5.

? 　　　　　**10 balls**

about　　　about　　　about
20　　　　　40　　　　　70

6.

? 　　　　　**10 flowers**

about　　　about　　　about
10　　　　　30　　　　　100

7.

? 　　　　　**10 pennies**

about　　　about　　　about
20　　　　　50　　　　　80

H.O.T. Problem

8. Critical Thinking Emily estimates that she needs 50 paper plates for her class picnic. There are 22 students in her class. Is Emily's estimate reasonable? Explain.

_____

_____

_____

Math at Home Activity: Look in the cupboard. Have your child estimate about how many cups there are.

Name _____

Write how many.

1.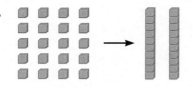

_____ ones = _____ tens

2.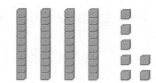

_____ tens _____ ones

_____ + _____ = _____

Circle the value of the **red** digit.

3. 72

7   or   70

4. 24

4   or   40

5. 39

3   or   30

Write each number or number name.

6. eighty-nine

_____

7. 15

_____

Estimate about how many. Circle the answer.

8.

about 20   about 40   about 80

?   10 peppers

---

9. Mrs. Andrews picked a number.
The digit in the tens place is a 7.
The digit in the ones place is more than 3
but less than 5.
What is the number?

_____

Circle the value of the **red** digit.

10. 29

  9 or 90

11. 32

  3 or 30

12. 64

  4 or 40

Write each number or number name.

13. ninety-three   **14.** fifty-two   **15.** 10

_____   _____   _____

Write how many.

16.

  ____ ones = ____ ten

17.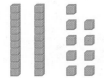

  ____ tens ____ ones

  ____ + ____ = ____

Estimate about how many. Circle the answer.

18.

  ?   **10 pickles**

about   about   about
30   50   80

19.

  ?   **10 grapes**

about   about   about
60   40   20

Formative Assessment

Name _____

Order Numbers

Main Idea

I will put numbers in order using a number line.

Vocabulary

number line

before

after

between

You can use a **number line** to order numbers.

Look at 5.
What comes just **before**?
What comes just **after**?

0 1 2 3 4 **5** 6 7 8 9 10 11 12 13 14 15

4 comes just before 5.

6 comes just after 5.

5 is **between** 4 and 6.   4, __5__ , 6

Check

Use the number line to fill in the blanks.

0 1 2 3 4 5 6 7 8 9 10 11 12 13 14 15

1. 10, _____, 12

2. 13, _____, 15

3. 7, _____, 9, _____

4. _____, 4, 5

5. 7, _____, 5

6. 15, _____, 13

---

7.  Choose four different two-digit numbers. Tell what you would do to put them in order. Order the numbers.

Use the number line to fill in the blanks.

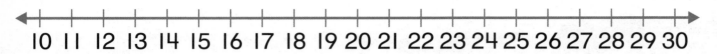

10 11 12 13 14 15 16 17 18 19 20 21 22 23 24 25 26 27 28 29 30

8. 21, _____, 23

9. _____, 12, 13

10. _____, 28, 29

11. _____, 12, 11

12. _____, 19, 20

13. _____, 20, 21, _____

14. _____, 13, 14

15. 25, _____, 27

16. 17, 18, _____, _____

17. 29, _____, 27

18. 28, 29, _____

19. 15, _____, 17

20. 13, 14, _____

21. 19, _____, 17

22. 10, _____, _____, 13

Data File

The NASA Glenn Research Center is in Cleveland, Ohio. Many people who work there study the use of computers in space travel. Computers can sort information very, very quickly.

23. Put this information in order: 1, 5, 9, 4. Write the numbers from least to greatest.

_____, _____, _____, _____

Math at Home Activity: Ask your child to name the number that comes between 24 and 26. Try other numbers and ask what comes before and after the number.

Name _____

Compare Numbers

Hands-On Activity

Get Ready

Main Idea

I will compare numbers using <, >, or =.

Vocabulary

compare

is greater than >

is less than <

is equal to =

Compare the tens. If the tens are equal, compare the ones.

You can use >, <, or = to **compare** numbers.

37 is greater than 24   37 ⬢ 24

32 is less than 35   32 ⬢ 35

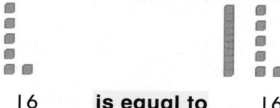

16 is equal to 16   16 ⬢ 16

Check

Compare. Write >, <, or =. Use  and ▪.

1. 54 ◯ 20

2. 31 ◯ 31

3. 42 ◯ 24

4. 63 ◯ 64

5. **Talk About It** How can you tell that 28 is greater than 26?

Remember
Compare the tens first.

Compare. Write >, <, or =. Use ▭▭▭▭▭▭ and ▪.

6.
23 ◯ 23

7.
30 ◯ 31

8. 81 ◯ 50

9. 92 ◯ 92

10. 25 ◯ 26

11. 77 ◯ 76

12. 89 ◯ 98

13. 55 ◯ 55

14. 21 ◯ 60

15. 64 ◯ 67

16. 49 ◯ 39

17. 0 ◯ 47

18. 80 ◯ 80

19. 42 ◯ 24

20. 70 ◯ 69

21. 15 ◯ 15

22. 38 ◯ 53

23. 20 ◯ 2

24. 30 ◯ 40

25. 29 ◯ 28

Problem Solving

26. Number Sense Manuel is scooping marbles into a bag at the toy store. Manuel's mother says he must take less than 25 marbles. Show the greatest number he can take.

_____ < 25

 Math at Home Activity: Ask your child to name two numbers greater than 52 and two numbers less than 52.

Name _____

Compare. Write <, >, or =.

49 ◯ 49

86 ◯ 68

28 ◯ 29

77 ◯ 71

33 ◯ 33

59 ◯ 69

42 ◯ 24

99 ◯ 99

65 ◯ 66

17 ◯ 16

75 ◯ 57

30 ◯ 40

98 ◯ 30

54 ◯ 54

25 ◯ 52

Chapter 1

Name the Price
Compare Numbers

You Will Need
- 1
- ♟ ♟

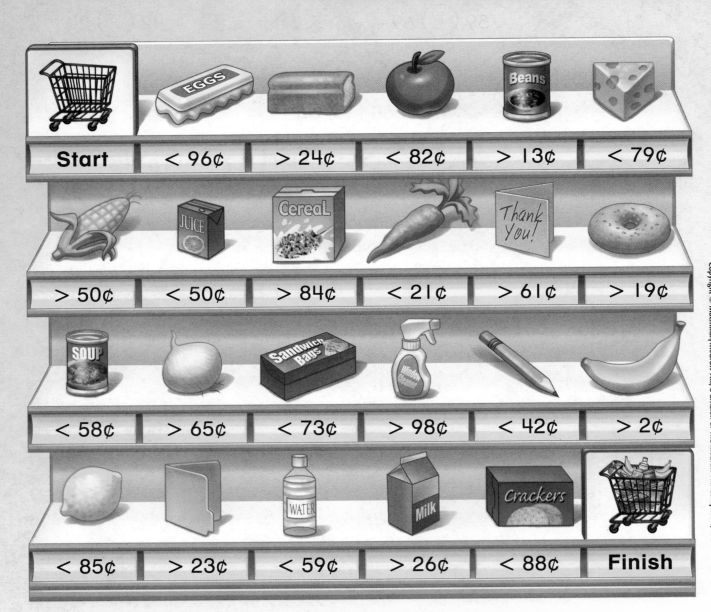

Start	< 96¢	> 24¢	< 82¢	> 13¢	< 79¢
> 50¢	< 50¢	> 84¢	< 21¢	> 61¢	> 19¢
< 58¢	> 65¢	< 73¢	> 98¢	< 42¢	> 2¢
< 85¢	> 23¢	< 59¢	> 26¢	< 88¢	Finish

Name _____

Patterns

Main Idea

I will show and describe patterns.

Vocabulary

pattern

Patterns are everywhere. Some **patterns** grow. They get bigger or smaller.

What comes next?

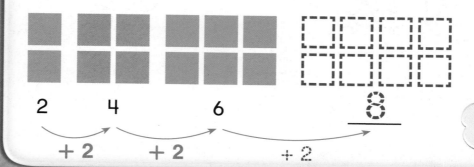

2   4   6   8

+ 2   + 2   + 2

2 is added to each number.

Check

Draw a picture to show what comes next in each growing pattern. Write the number of shapes.

1.

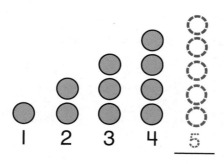

1   2   3   4   5

2.

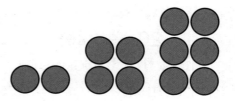

6   5   4   ___

3.

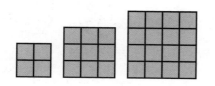

___

4.

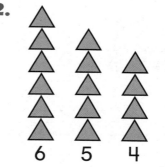

___

5. **Talk About It** Look at Exercise 3. Describe the growing pattern.

Write what comes next in each growing pattern.

6. 5, 10, 15, 20, ___, ___, ___

7. 10, 20, 30, ___, 50, ___, ___, 80

Draw a picture to show what comes next in each growing pattern. Write the number of shapes.

8.

___ ___ ___ ___

9.

___ ___ ___ ___

10.

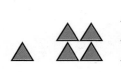

3   6   10   ___

11.

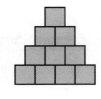

1   4   9   ___

Problem Solving

12. Visual Thinking Amy saved 10 pennies the first week, 20 pennies the second week, and 30 pennies the third week. If this growing pattern continues for six weeks, how many pennies will Amy have in all?

_____ pennies

Math at Home Activity: Ask your child to create a repeating pattern and a growing pattern using cereal.

Problem-Solving Investigation

Main Idea

I will choose a strategy to solve the problem.

I have a collection of rocks. I put 1 on the top shelf, 3 on the second shelf, and 5 on the third shelf. If I put rocks on the next two shelves in the same pattern, how many rocks will be on the shelves in all?

Your Mission: Find how many rocks are on the shelves.

Understand

What do I need to find?
Circle the question.

Plan

How will I solve the problem?

Solve

One way is to draw a picture.

_____ rocks in all

Check

Look back.
Is my answer reasonable?

Mixed Problem Solving

Problem-Solving Strategies

- Draw a picture
- Act it out
- Use logical reasoning

Choose a strategy. Solve.

1. There are three pigs in the barn.
   Two chickens go into the barn.
   How many animals are in the barn?

_____ animals

2. The water ride is open. Five log boats
   are being used. I child is in the first boat.
   3 children are in the second boat. 5 are in
   the third boat. If this growing pattern continues,
   how many children will be in the fifth boat?

_____ children

3. Mrs. Walker's class is collecting cans to recycle.
   Jeff brought 10 cans, and Liza brought 8 cans.
   How many cans did Jeff and Liza bring?

_____ cans

4. My number is greater than 41.
   It is less than 49.
   It has a 7 in the ones place.
   What is my number?

_____

Math at Home Activity: Take advantage of problem-solving opportunities during daily routines such as riding in the car, bedtime, doing laundry, putting away groceries, planning schedules, and so on.

Patterns on a Hundred Chart

Get Ready

Main Idea

I will skip count to create patterns on a hundred chart.

Vocabulary

skip count

You can use patterns to count. This is called **skip counting**. You can skip count by 2s to count pairs of shoes.

2   4   6   8   10

1	2	3	4	5	6	7	8	9	10
11	12	13	14	15	16	17	18	19	20
21	22	23	24	25	26	27	28	29	30
31	32	33	34	35	36	37	38	39	40
41	42	43	44	45	46	47	48	49	50
51	52	53	54	55	56	57	58	59	60

Skip counting by 2s on a hundred chart produces patterns.

Check

Use the hundred chart.

1. Skip count by 2s. Color the numbers blue. Start on 2.

2. Skip count by 5s. Circle the numbers. Start on 5.

3. Skip count by 10s. Draw a line under the numbers. Start on 10.

4. **Talk About It** What patterns did you make in the hundred chart?

1	2	3	4	5	6	7	8	9	10
11	12	13	14	15	16	17	18	19	20
21	22	23	24	25	26	27	28	29	30
31	32	33	34	35	36	37	38	39	40
41	42	43	44	45	46	47	48	49	50
51	52	53	54	55	56	57	58	59	60
61	62	63	64	65	66	67	68	69	70
71	72	73	74	75	76	77	78	79	80
81	82	83	84	85	86	87	88	89	90
91	92	93	94	95	96	97	98	99	100

Use the hundred chart.

1	2	3	4	5	6	7	8	9	10
11	12	13	14	15	16	17	18	19	20
21	22	23	24	25	26	27	28	29	30
31	32	33	34	35	36	37	38	39	40
41	42	43	44	45	46	47	48	49	50
51	52	53	54	55	56	57	58	59	60
61	62	63	64	65	66	67	68	69	70
71	72	73	74	75	76	77	78	79	80
81	82	83	84	85	86	87	88	89	90
91	92	93	94	95	96	97	98	99	100

5. Count by 2s.

2, 4, 6, 8, _____, _____, _____, _____

6. Count by 4s.

12, 16, 20, 24, _____, _____, _____, _____

Write the missing numbers. Describe the pattern.

7. 34, 36, 38, _____

   skip counting by _____

8. 10, _____, 30, 40

   skip counting by _____

9. 55, 58, _____, 64

   skip counting by _____

10. 75, _____, _____, 90

   skip counting by _____

Problem Solving

Number Sense

11. There are 6 gloves. Each glove has 5 fingers. How many fingers are there in all?

_____ fingers

12. There are 20 wheels on a group of bicycles. Each bicycle has 2 wheels. How many bicycles are there?

_____ bicycles

Math at Home Activity: Ask your child to skip count out loud by twos, threes, and fives.

D

What do you celebrate?
What special events do
you dress up for?

Draw a mask you could wear.

FOLD DOWN

Problem Solving
in Social Studies

Real-World MATH

Some people dress up for
celebrations. This is an African
mask used in a special ceremony.

This book belongs to

_____

A

This is a mask from Japan.
It is over 1,000 years old!

These masks are from Mexico.

This mask is about 25 years old.

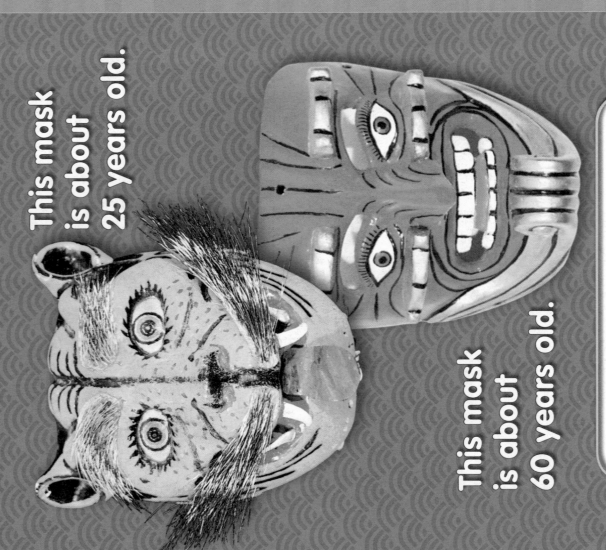

This mask is about 60 years old.

Put an X on the mask on this page that is older.

Name _____

Vocabulary

Draw lines to match.

1. digit

2. number line

3. is greater than

4. is less than

a. 23 > 20

b. 2

c.
    27 28 29 30

d. 7 < 8

Concepts

Estimate about how many. Circle the answer.

5.

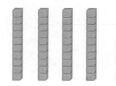

?   **10 marbles**

about
10

about
30

about
90

Write how many tens and ones. Then write the number.

6.

_____ tens _____ ones

_____ + _____ = _____

7.

_____ ten _____ ones

_____ + _____ = _____

Circle the value of the **red** digit.

8. 45   4 or 40

9. 75   5 or 50

Write each number or number name.

10. ninety-three _____

11. 10 _____

Use the number line to fill in the blanks.

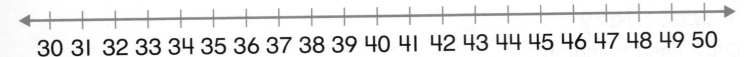

30 31 32 33 34 35 36 37 38 39 40 41 42 43 44 45 46 47 48 49 50

12. 42, _____, 44   **13.** 46, _____, 48, _____   **14.** 33, _____, 31

Compare. Write >, <, or =.

15. 51 ◯ 57   **16.** 94 ◯ 91   **17.** 33 ◯ 33   **18.** 49 ◯ 59

Draw a picture to show what comes next in the growing pattern. Write the number of shapes.

19.

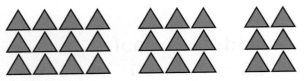

___   ___   ___   ___

Write the missing numbers. Describe the pattern.

20. 74, _____, 78, 80

skip counting by _____

21. 35, _____, 45, _____

skip counting by _____

Problem Solving

22. What is Sophia's address?
There are 3 tens. There are
more tens than ones.

Sophia's address is _____.

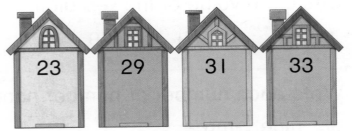

23   29   31   33

Summative Assessment

Name _____

Listen as your teacher reads each problem.
Choose the correct answer.

1. There are 53 crayons in a jar. How many tens and ones are there in 53?

5 tens 3 ones ◯   3 tens 5 ones ◯

5 tens 0 ones ◯   3 tens 1 one ◯

2. Look at the groups of numbers. Find the group of numbers that is in order from least to greatest.

(28, 31, 30) ◯   (28, 30, 31) ◯

(31, 30, 28) ◯   (30, 31, 28) ◯

3. Which number comes after 76?

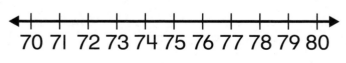
70 71 72 73 74 75 76 77 78 79 80

67 ◯   73 ◯   75 ◯   77 ◯

4. Look at the pattern of numbers. Find the number that comes next in the pattern.

(78, 68, 58, _____)

38 ◯   42 ◯   48 ◯   84 ◯

5. Which of these shows the number of apples?

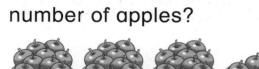

10 + 10 ◯   3 + 3 + 3 + 1 ◯

10 + 10 + 10 + 4 ◯   1 + 1 + 1 + 1 ◯

6. What is another way to write eighty-nine?

8 + 9 ◯   40 + 9 ◯

90 + 8 ◯   80 + 9 ◯

7. Which number sentence is true?

56 = 45 ⚪

56 < 45 ⚪

56 < 54 ⚪

56 > 45 ⚪

8. What number is 40 more than 11?

1	2	3	4	5	6	7	8	9	10
⑪	12	13	14	15	16	17	18	19	20
21	22	23	24	25	26	27	28	29	30
31	32	33	34	35	36	37	38	39	40
41	42	43	44	45	46	47	48	49	50
51	52	53	54	55	56	57	58	59	60

7 ⚪   15 ⚪   31 ⚪   51 ⚪

9. What is the place value of the four in eighty-four?

4 ⚪

8 ⚪

40 ⚪

80 ⚪

10. Which of these shows the number name for 14?

forty ⚪

fifteen ⚪

fourteen ⚪

four ⚪

11. Look at the table. There are 6 eggs in a carton. How many eggs are there in 4 cartons?

Eggs	
Number of Cartons	Number of Eggs
1	6
2	12
3	18
4	

_____ eggs

12. Gina is counting her socks. She has 5 pairs of socks. How many socks does she have in all?

_____ socks

Summative Assessment

Apply Addition Concepts

Key Vocabulary

add

addend

sum

doubles

Explore

Look at the picture. How could you find how many there are?

Name _____

Are You Ready for Chapter 2?

Write the number of objects.

1.

_____

2.

_____

Add.

3.  + ⬤⬤⬤⬤

_____ oranges

4.

_____ bananas

5. ◯◯◯◯◯◯⬤

7 + 1 = _____

6. ◯◯◯⬤⬤⬤⬤

3 + 4 = _____

Look at the picture. Write the number sentence. Add.

7.

_____ + _____ = _____ apples

Solve.

8. There are 2 flies and 1 spider in a spider web.
How many bugs are there in all?

_____ bugs

This page checks skills needed for Chapter 2.

MATH at HOME

Dear Family,

Today my class started Chapter 2, **Apply Addition Concepts**. In this chapter, I will learn to use different strategies to solve addition problems. Here is an activity we can do and a list of books we can read together.

Love,

_____

Activity

Have your child count the number of pictures on each page of the newspaper. How many more pictures would there need to be to reach 10?

Key Vocabulary

addend any numbers or quantities being added together $6 + 2 = 8$

addend ⬑   ⬏ addend

doubles two addends that are the same number $3 + 3 = 6$

Math Online ⟩ Click on the eGlossary link at <u>macmillanmh.com</u> to find out more about these words. There are 13 languages.

Books to Read

The 512 Ants on Sullivan Street
by Carol A. Losi
Cartwheel Books, 1997.

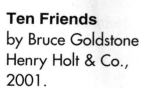

The King's Chessboard
by David Birch
Puffin, 1993.

Ten Friends
by Bruce Goldstone
Henry Holt & Co., 2001.

Estimada familia:

Hoy mi clase comenzó el Capítulo 2, **Desarrolla conceptos de suma**. En este capítulo, aprenderé a usar diferentes estrategias para resolver problemas de suma. A continuación, hay una actividad que podemos hacer y una lista de libros que podemos leer juntos.

Cariños,

_____

Actividad

Pídanle a su hijo(a) que cuente el número de imágenes en cada página del periódico. ¿Cuántas imágenes adicionales se necesitan para llegar hasta 10?

Vocabulario clave

sumando cualquier número o cantidad que se suma

$$6 + 2 = 8$$

sumando ↑ ↑ sumando

dobles dos adendos idénticos $3 + 3 = 6$

Math Online Visiten el enlace eGlossary en macmillanmh.com para averiguar más sobre estas palabras, las cuales se muestran en 13 idiomas.

Libros recomendados

Sumar y contar hacia adelante
de Diyan Leake
Heinemann, 2006.

Puedo sumar
de Garry Price
Publicaciones Citem
sa de cv, 2002.

Name _____

Addition Properties

Get Ready

Main Idea

I will add zero and add in any order to find sums.

Vocabulary

add

addend

sum

You **add** to find a sum. The numbers you add are called **addends**. The answer is the **sum**.

You can add numbers in any order. The sum is the same. This is the Commutative Property.

$3 + 5 = $ **8** $5 + 3 = $ **8**

↑ ↑   ↑
addends   sum

When you add zero to a number, the sum is always that number.

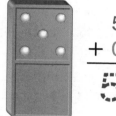

$$\begin{array}{r} 5 \\ + 0 \\ \hline 5 \end{array}$$ ← addends ← sum

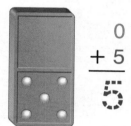

$$\begin{array}{r} 0 \\ + 5 \\ \hline 5 \end{array}$$

Check

Find each sum.

1.

$4 + 3 = $ **7**

$3 + 4 = $ **7**

2.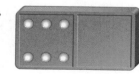

$6 + 0 = $ _____

$0 + 6 = $ _____

3.

$$\begin{array}{r} 2 \\ + 4 \\ \hline \end{array} \qquad \begin{array}{r} 4 \\ + 2 \\ \hline \end{array}$$

4.

$$\begin{array}{r} 2 \\ + 5 \\ \hline \end{array} \qquad \begin{array}{r} 5 \\ + 2 \\ \hline \end{array}$$

5. **Talk About It** Why is the sum the same when you find $3 + 2$ or $2 + 3$?

Use counters. Find each sum.

6.

$5 + 1 =$ _____

$1 + 5 =$ _____

7.

5	4
+ 4	+ 5

8.	0	3	**9.**	6	3	**10.**	7	1
	+ 3	+ 0		+ 3	+ 6		+ 1	+ 7

11. $6 + 2 =$ _____

$2 + 6 =$ _____

12. $8 + 0 =$ _____

$0 + 8 =$ _____

13. $4 + 2 =$ _____

$2 + 4 =$ _____

14. $3 + 4 =$ _____

$4 + 3 =$ _____

15. $0 + 9 =$ _____

$9 + 0 =$ _____

16. $8 + 1 =$ _____

$1 + 8 =$ _____

H.O.T. Problems

Algebra Write the missing numbers.

17. $4 + \boxed{} = 3 + 4$ **18.** $1 + 6 = 6 + \boxed{}$

19. $7 + 2 = \boxed{} + 7$ **20.** $\boxed{} + 5 = 5 + 0$

 Math at Home Activity: Using objects in the house, have your child show one group of 2 and one group of 3. Have your child tell you two addition sentences about the objects.

Name _____

Count On to Add

Get Ready

Main Idea

I will use a number line to count on to add.

Vocabulary

count on

Review Vocabulary

addend

Use a number line to **count on** to add.
Find 3 + 7. Start with the greater addend.

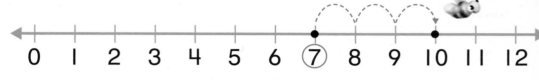

0 1 2 3 4 5 6 ⑦ 8 9 10 11 12

Start at 7. Count on 3.

3 + 7 = 10
and 10 = 3 + 7
are the same.

$3 + 7 = \underline{10}$

$\underline{10} = 3 + 7$

Check

Think
Start with the greater number and count on.

Count on to add. Use the number line to help.

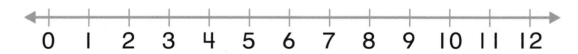

0 1 2 3 4 5 6 7 8 9 10 11 12

1. $6 + 3 = \underline{9}$

2. $4 + 2 = \underline{\hphantom{00}}$

3. $5 + 3 = \underline{\hphantom{00}}$

4. $2 + 9 = \underline{\hphantom{00}}$

5. $1 + 3 = \underline{\hphantom{00}}$

6. $6 + 2 = \underline{\hphantom{00}}$

7. $\underline{\hphantom{00}} = 2 + 7$

8. $\underline{\hphantom{00}} = 9 + 1$

9. $\underline{\hphantom{00}} = 4 + 3$

10. **Talk About It** Why should you count on from the greater addend?

Count on to add. Use the number line to help.

0 I 2 3 4 5 6 7 8 9 10 11 12

11. _____ = 5 + 2

12. 7 + I = _____

13. 3 + 5 = _____

14. 3 + 8 = _____

15. 6 + I = _____

16. _____ = 3 + 4

17. _____ = 9 + 3

18. 2 + 8 = _____

19. 7 + 3 = _____

Remember your facts. Add as quickly as you can.

20. 2
    + 7
    ----

21. 3
    + 2
    ----

22. I
    + 9
    ----

23. 5
    + I
    ----

24. 2
    + 4
    ----

25. 3
    + 6
    ----

26. I
    + 4
    ----

27. 3
    + I
    ----

28. 2
    + 6
    ----

29. 9
    + 2
    ----

30. 8
    + I
    ----

31. 4
    + 3
    ----

32. 2
    + 8
    ----

33. 2
    + 5
    ----

34. 3
    + 7
    ----

35. 3
    + 9
    ----

36. 2
    + 5
    ----

37. 6
    + 3
    ----

38. 2
    + 3
    ----

39. 4
    + 3

GO on

Name _____

Practice with Technology

You can use a to count on.

RULE: Count on 2.

Press.

Use your calculator to add.

ON/OFF	6	6

+ 2 = 8

+ 2 = 10

+ 2 = 12

---

40. RULE: Count on 3.

Press.

ON/OFF	9	9

+ 3 =

+ 3 =

+ 3 =

+ 3 =

---

41. RULE: Count on 1.

Press.

ON/OFF	2	2

+ 1 =

+ 1 =

+ 1 =

+ 1 =

42. **RULE: Count on 3.**

Press.

+ 3 = [ ]

+ 3 = [ ]

+ 3 = [ ]

+ 3 = [ ]

+ 3 = [ ]

+ 3 = [ ]

+ 3 = [ ]

43. **RULE: Count on 2.**

Press.

+ 2 = [ ]

+ 2 = [ ]

+ 2 = [ ]

+ 2 = [ ]

+ 2 = [ ]

+ 2 = [ ]

+ 2 = [ ]

44.  **WRITING IN ►MATH** How does counting on help you add?

_____

_____

_____

_____

Math at Home Activity: Give your child an addition fact. Have him or her count on from the greater number to find the sum.

Name _____

Problem-Solving Strategy
Act It Out

Main Idea

I will act out the problem to solve it.

Harold sold all of the green peppers and all of the onions. How many vegetables did Harold sell?

Vegetables For Sale

Understand

What do I need to find?
Circle the question.

Plan

How will I solve the problem?

Solve

Act it out with models.

_____ vegetables

Check

Look back.
Is my answer reasonable?

Try It

Act it out with models.

1. There are 8 ants on the ant hill.
2 more ants come.
How many ants are there now?

_____ ants

---

2. 3 ladybugs climb onto a leaf.
8 more join them.
How many ladybugs are on the leaf?

_____ ladybugs

Your Turn

Act it out with models.

3. 7 butterflies are on a flower.
2 more land on the flower.
How many butterflies are on the flower now?

_____ butterflies

---

4. 9 bees are in a hive.
0 bees join them.
How many bees are there in all?

_____ bees

Math at Home Activity: Tell a simple addition problem.
Have your child use objects such as dry cereal or beans to solve
the problem.

Name _____

Doubles

Get Ready

Main Idea

I will use doubles facts to find sums.

Vocabulary

doubles

Review Vocabulary

sum

Two addends that are the same are called **doubles**.

Use doubles facts to find the sum.

6 + 6 = 12

↑ addend   ↑ addend   ↑ sum

Check

Add. Use cubes to help.

1.

4 + 4 = __8__

2.

3 + 3 = _____

3. 5 + 5 = _____

4. 9 + 9 = _____

5. 7 + 7 = _____

6. 8 + 8 = _____

7. **Talk About It** How do you remember 5 + 5? 2 + 2?

Add. Circle the doubles facts.

8.　　0
　　+ 0

9.　　7
　　+ 1

10.　　2
　　+ 8

11.　　8
　　+ 8

12.　　3
　　+ 6

13.　　7
　　+ 3

14.　　8
　　+ 3

15.　　5
　　+ 2

16.　　2
　　+ 9

17.　　4
　　+ 4

18.　　6
　　+ 6

19.　　3
　　+ 3

20.　　2
　　+ 2

21.　　7
　　+ 7

22.　　1
　　+ 1

23.　　9
　　+ 3

24.　　7
　　+ 2

25.　　9
　　+ 9

Problem Solving

Number Sense ✏️ Draw ▶ a picture to solve.
Write the number sentence.

26. Andy has 3 dogs. Chris has the same number of dogs. How many dogs do they have altogether?

_____ + _____ = _____

_____ dogs

🏠 **Math at Home Activity:** Have your child use objects to make doubles and tell the addition fact.

Name _____

Find the sum.

1.
```
    2
  + 1
  ___
```

2.
```
    4
  + 4
  ___
```

3.
```
    5
  + 2
  ___
```

4.
```
    8
  + 8
  ___
```

5.
```
    8
  + 3
  ___
```

6.
```
    5
  + 5
  ___
```

7.
```
    2
  + 7
  ___
```

8.
```
    5
  + 3
  ___
```

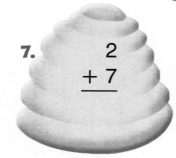

9.
```
    9
  + 9
  ___
```

10.
```
    4
  + 2
  ___
```

11.
```
    3
  + 7
  ___
```

12.
```
    4
  + 3
  ___
```

13.
```
    3
  + 3
  ___
```

14.
```
    4
  + 4
  ___
```

15.
```
    5
  + 5
  ___
```

16.
```
    6
  + 6
  ___
```

Packing for a Picnic
Doubles

You Will Need

 1

 2

 6

 8

 10

 12

Play with a partner. Take turns.

- Put your ♟ on Start.
- Flip the ⬤.
- Move your ♟ 1 space for red or 2 spaces for yellow.
- Which addends can you double to get the number on the space?
- Find the picnic item that matches the addends.
- Draw that item in your picnic basket.
- Play until someone reaches Finish.

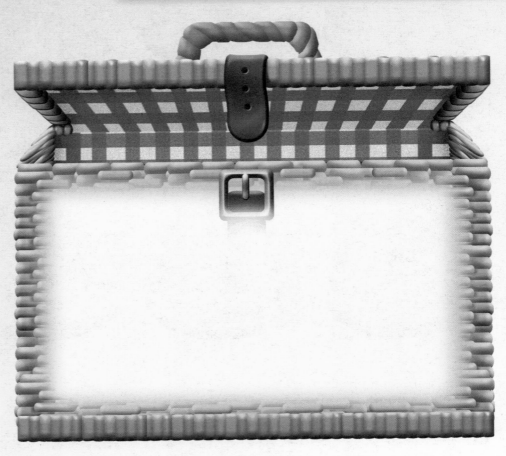

Start	16	4	2	24	Lose a Turn	12	20	Finish

Near Doubles

Get Ready

Main Idea

I will use doubles facts to find other sums.

Review Vocabulary

doubles

Doubles facts can help you to learn other facts. If you know $6 + 6 = 12$, you can find $6 + 7$ and $6 + 5$.

$6 + 6 = \underline{12}$

doubles

$6 + 7 = \underline{13}$

doubles plus 1

$6 + 5 = \underline{11}$

doubles minus 1

Check

Find each sum. Use cubes to help.

1.

$\underline{3} + \underline{3} = \underline{6}$

$\underline{3} + \underline{4} = \underline{7}$

2. $7 + 7 = \underline{\hspace{1cm}}$

$7 + 8 = \underline{\hspace{1cm}}$

3. $2 + 2 = \underline{\hspace{1cm}}$

$2 + 1 = \underline{\hspace{1cm}}$

4. $5 + 5 = \underline{\hspace{1cm}}$

$5 + 6 = \underline{\hspace{1cm}}$

5. $9 + 9 = \underline{\hspace{1cm}}$

$9 + 8 = \underline{\hspace{1cm}}$

6. **Talk About It** How does knowing doubles help you learn doubles plus 1 or doubles minus 1?

Practice

Find each sum. Use cubes to help.

> I know 4 + 4 = 8. That helps me know 4 + 5. The sum is one more.

7. 4 + 4 = _____

8. 4 + 5 = _____

9. 1 + 1 = _____

10. 1 + 2 = _____

11. 4 + 3 = _____

12. 8 + 8 = _____

13. 0 + 0 = _____

14. 5 + 6 = _____

15. 7
   + 8
   ___

16. 7
   + 7
   ___

17. 6
   + 6
   ___

18. 3
   + 2
   ___

19. 4
   + 3
   ___

20. 8
   + 7
   ___

21. 5
   + 4
   ___

22. 7
   + 6
   ___

23. 9
   + 9
   ___

24. 8
   + 9
   ___

25. 6
   + 5
   ___

26. 8
   + 8
   ___

Problem Solving

Number Sense

27. What doubles facts can help you solve 7 + 8?

_____ + _____ = _____

or _____ + _____ = _____

7 + 8 = _____

28. What doubles facts can help you solve 5 + 6?

_____ + _____ = _____

or _____ + _____ = _____

5 + 6 = _____

Math at Home Activity: Ask your child what the doubles-plus-one fact would be for 4 + 4.

Name _____

Find each sum.

1.   5   1
   + 1   + 5

2.   7   0
   + 0   + 7

Count on to add. Use the number line to help.

1   2   3   4   5   6   7   8   9   10   11   12   13   14   15   16   17   18   19   20

3. $10 + 3 =$ _____

4. $1 + 3 =$ _____

Add. Circle the doubles facts.

5.   0
   + 3

6.   1
   + 1

7.   3
   + 6

8.   9
   + 9

9.   6
   + 4

10.   9
   + 8

11.   7
   + 6

12.   4
   + 5

13.   8
   + 8

14.   5
   + 5

Solve.

15. Carla picked 6 daisies. Daniel picked 7 daisies.
How many daisies did they pick?

_____ + _____ = _____

_____ daisies

Spiral Review

Chapters 1–2

Circle the value of the **red** digit.

16. 19

  1   or   10

17. 63

  3   or   30

18. 40

  4   or   40

Compare. Write >, <, or =.

19. 13 ◯ 31

20. 90 ◯ 89

21. 26 ◯ 42

22. 73 ◯ 73

Fill in the blank.

23. 69, _____, 71

24. 48, _____, 50

Find each sum.

25. 4 + 5 = _____

26. 5 + 6 = _____

Write the missing numbers. Then describe the pattern.

27. 53, 56, _____, 62

skip counting by _____

28. 30, _____, 50, _____

skip counting by _____

Add. Circle the doubles facts.

29. 8 + 2 = _____

30. 6 + 6 = _____

31. 3 + 2 = _____

32. 7 + 6 = _____

33. 3 + 8 = _____

34. 7 + 7 = _____

70 seventy

Formative Assessment

Copyright © Macmillan/McGraw-Hill, a division of The McGraw-Hill Companies, Inc.

Name _____

Make a 10

Hands-On
Activity

Get Ready

Main Idea

I will make a ten to solve addition problems.

You can make a ten to help you add. Find $8 + 4$.

First:
Show 8.
Then show 4.

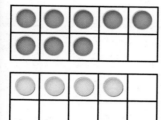

Next:
Move 2 counters to make a 10.

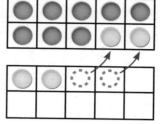

Show $8 + 4$ as $10 + 2$.

Last:
Add.

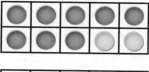
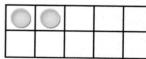

$8 + 4 = \underline{12}$

Check

Use WorkMat 1 and . Add.

1. $9 + 5 = \underline{14}$

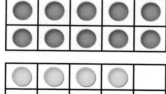
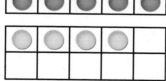

2. $7 + 5 = \underline{\hphantom{00}}$

3. $8 + 5 = \underline{\hphantom{00}}$

4. $6 + 5 = \underline{\hphantom{00}}$

5. $6 + 8 = \underline{\hphantom{00}}$

6. $4 + 9 = \underline{\hphantom{00}}$

7. $8 + 4 = \underline{\hphantom{00}}$

8. $4 + 6 = \underline{\hphantom{00}}$

9. $2 + 9 = \underline{\hphantom{00}}$

10. **Talk About It** How does making a ten help you add?

 **Practice**

> **Remember**
> Make a ten, count on, or find doubles to add.

Use WorkMat I and . Add.

11. 9 + 4 = _____   **12.** 7 + 7 = _____   **13.** 9 + 7 = _____

14. 4 + 8 = _____   **15.** 8 + 9 = _____   **16.** 6 + 8 = _____

17. 3 + 9 = _____   **18.** 7 + 5 = _____   **19.** 4 + 6 = _____

20. 3   **21.** 4   **22.** 2   **23.** 7   **24.** 8   **25.** 1
  + 7   + 9   + 9   + 8   + 8   + 9

26. 9   **27.** 2   **28.** 3   **29.** 4   **30.** 6   **31.** 7
  + 9   + 8   + 9   + 7   + 9   + 3

H.O.T. Problem

32. Algebra Write the missing numbers.
What pattern do you see? Explain the pattern.

| 10 | + | 0 | = | 9 | + | 1 |

| 10 | + | 1 | = | 9 | + | 2 | _____

| 10 | + | ☐ | = | ☐ | + | 3 | _____

| 10 | + | ☐ | = | ☐ | + | ☐ | _____

| ☐ | + | ☐ | = | ☐ | + | ☐ | _____

Math at Home Activity: Ask your child to tell you how to use a ten-frame to add 8 + 7.

Name _____

Add Three Numbers

Get Ready

Main Idea

I will group addends in different ways to make the sum easier to find.

You can group addends in different ways. The sum is the same.

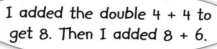

I added the double 4 + 4 to get 8. Then I added 8 + 6.

I added 4 + 6 to make 10. Then I added 10 + 4.

$$
\begin{array}{r}
4 \\
6 \rightarrow \boxed{8} \\
+\ 4 \\
\hline
8 \\
+\ 6 \\
\hline
14
\end{array}
\qquad
\begin{array}{r}
4 \\
6 \rightarrow \boxed{10} \\
+\ 4 \\
\hline
10 \\
+\ 4 \\
\hline
14
\end{array}
$$

✓ Check

Remember
You can add numbers in different ways and get the same sum. This is the Associative Property.

Find each sum. Circle the numbers you add first. Write that sum in the box.

1.
$$
\begin{array}{r}
⑦ \\
4 \\
+\ ⑦
\end{array}
\rightarrow \boxed{14}
$$
18

2.
$$
\begin{array}{r}
⑨ \\
① \\
+\ 2
\end{array}
\quad \boxed{}
$$

3.
$$
\begin{array}{r}
3 \\
9 \\
+\ 3
\end{array}
\quad \boxed{}
$$

4.
$$
\begin{array}{r}
2 \\
4 \\
+\ 2
\end{array}
\quad \boxed{}
$$

5.
$$
\begin{array}{r}
2 \\
7 \\
+\ 8
\end{array}
\quad \boxed{}
$$

6.
$$
\begin{array}{r}
1 \\
6 \\
+\ 9
\end{array}
\quad \boxed{}
$$

7. **Talk About It** How did you decide which numbers to add first in Exercise 6?

Find each sum.

8. 4 + 3 + 4 = _____

9. 4 + 3 + 7 = _____

10. 2 + 8 + 3 = _____

11. 6 + 1 + 6 = _____

12. 5 + 5 + 5 = _____

13. 6 + 6 + 3 = _____

14. 7 + 4 + 7 = _____

15. 9 + 8 + 1 = _____

Remember
Add two numbers first. Look for facts you know.

16.
```
   1
   7
+  3
____
```

17.
```
   5
   7
+  5
____
```

18.
```
   3
   5
+  7
____
```

19.
```
   7
   7
+  1
____
```

20.
```
   9
   8
+  1
____
```

21.
```
   2
   2
+  8
____
```

22.
```
   6
   6
+  5
____
```

23.
```
   8
   4
+  6
____
```

Data File

Grand Canyon National Park Activities	
Activity	People
Hike	7
Fish	4
Camp	4
Ride Horses	3

24. How many people went fishing, went camping, and rode horses? _____

25. How many people rode horses, went hiking, and went fishing? _____

Math at Home Activity: Have your child show you how to add 7 + 7 + 1.

Name _____

Problem-Solving Investigation

Main Idea

I will choose a problem-solving strategy to solve problems.

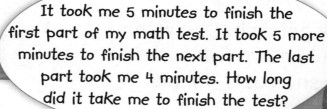

It took me 5 minutes to finish the first part of my math test. It took 5 more minutes to finish the next part. The last part took me 4 minutes. How long did it take me to finish the test?

Your Mission:
Find out how long the math test took Joe to finish.

Understand

What do I need to find?
Circle the question.

Plan

How will I solve the problem?

Solve

One way is to draw a picture.

Joe will finish in _____ minutes.

Check

Look back.
Is my answer reasonable?

Mixed Problem Solving

Choose a strategy. Solve.

Problem-Solving Strategies

• Draw a picture
• Use logical reasoning
• Act it out

1. Maria has 9 goldfish. She wants to put them into two fish tanks. Find a way she could do this.

2. Steve, Elena and Ian are playing with toy airplanes. Steve gives 8 planes to Ian and 8 to Elena. He has 2 airplanes left. How many airplanes did he start with?

_____ planes

3. The library has 4 books about brown bears. They have 3 books about black bears. There is 1 fewer book about polar bears than black bears. How many books about bears are there altogether?

_____ books

4. Arielle has 4 markers. Julia has 3 more markers than Arielle. How many markers do they have in all?

_____ markers

Math at Home Activity: Take advantage of problem-solving opportunities during daily routines such as riding in the car, bedtime, doing laundry, putting away groceries, planning schedules, and so on.

Raspberries grow on bushes.

What is your favorite fruit?

Where does it grow?

FOLD DOWN

Problem Solving in Science

Real-World MATH

Fruit grows in different places.
Oranges grow on trees.

This book belongs to

Watermelons grow on a vine. There are many watermelons on each vine.

Alex saved some seeds from last year's watermelons and planted them.

Alex has 3 watermelon vines. Each vine has 5 watermelons. Draw a picture to find out how many watermelons Alex has.

_____ watermelons

Name _____

Vocabulary

Circle the right answer.

1. **sum**	2. **doubles**	3. **add**

$6 + 5$ $5 + 5 = 10$ $6 + 3$ $4 + 4$ $5 + 1$ $5 - 1$

Concepts

Count on to add. Use the number line to help.

1 2 3 4 5 6 7 8 9 10 11 12 13 14 15 16 17 18 19 20

4. $\begin{array}{r} 8 \\ +2 \\ \hline \end{array}$ $\begin{array}{r} 2 \\ +8 \\ \hline \end{array}$
5. $\begin{array}{r} 4 \\ +3 \\ \hline \end{array}$ $\begin{array}{r} 3 \\ +4 \\ \hline \end{array}$
6. $\begin{array}{r} 9 \\ +1 \\ \hline \end{array}$ $\begin{array}{r} 1 \\ +9 \\ \hline \end{array}$

Find each sum.

7. $9 + 5 =$ _____
8. $7 + 4 =$ _____
9. $6 + 5 =$ _____

Add. Circle the doubles facts.

10. $\begin{array}{r} 2 \\ +3 \\ \hline \end{array}$
11. $\begin{array}{r} 1 \\ +2 \\ \hline \end{array}$
12. $\begin{array}{r} 7 \\ +7 \\ \hline \end{array}$
13. $\begin{array}{r} 7 \\ +6 \\ \hline \end{array}$
14. $\begin{array}{r} 5 \\ +4 \\ \hline \end{array}$
15. $\begin{array}{r} 3 \\ +4 \\ \hline \end{array}$

16. $4 + 5 =$ _____
17. $9 + 8 =$ _____
18. $0 + 0 =$ _____

Add.

19. 8 + 7 = _____   **20.** 7 + 6 = _____   **21.** 9 + 3 = _____

Find each sum. Circle the numbers you add first.

22. 2 + 8 + 4 = _____   **23.** 5 + 1 + 5 = _____

24. 6 + 4 + 6 = _____   **25.** 7 + 8 + 3 = _____

26. $\begin{array}{r} 5 \\ 3 \\ + 5 \\ \hline \end{array}$ **27.** $\begin{array}{r} 1 \\ 6 \\ + 4 \\ \hline \end{array}$ **28.** $\begin{array}{r} 3 \\ 9 \\ + 1 \\ \hline \end{array}$ **29.** $\begin{array}{r} 8 \\ 8 \\ + 1 \\ \hline \end{array}$

Problem Solving

30. Roderick, Carlo, and Ty are playing with baseballs. Roderick throws 5 to Carlo and 5 to Ty. He has 6 baseballs left. How many baseballs did he start with?

_____ baseballs

31. Shani walks the dogs in her neighborhood. One neighbor has 3 dogs. Another neighbor has 4 dogs. How many dogs does she walk?

_____ dogs

Summative Assessment

Name _____

Listen as your teacher reads each problem.
Choose the correct answer.

1. A kite costs $9. A roll of string costs $4. What is the total cost of both items?

$5	$12	$13	$14
○	○	○	○

4. Use the number line to count on. What is the sum?

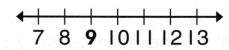

7 8 **9** 10 11 12 13

$9 + 3 = $ _____

15	12	10	6
○	○	○	○

2. What number goes in the box to make this number sentence true?

$$0 + 3 = \boxed{} + 0$$

0	3	4	6
○	○	○	○

5. What number is between 73 and 76?

$$73 < \boxed{} < 76$$

72	73	75	77
○	○	○	○

3. There are 31 days in January. Which of the following groups of cubes shows 31?

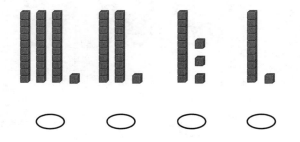

○	○	○	○

6. Which doubles fact has the same sum as 9 + 5?

6 + 6	5 + 5	7 + 7	6 + 7
○	○	○	○

7. A number has four tens and six ones. What is the number?

6   16   46   64

◯   ◯   ◯   ◯

8. Look at the number sentence below. Which number sentence is in the same fact family?

$$8 + 6 = 14$$

$8 - 6 = 2$ $14 + 6 = 20$

◯   ◯

$8 + 4 = 12$ $6 + 8 = 14$

◯   ◯

9. Tory has 7 tomatoes. She picks 7 more. How many tomatoes does Tory have?

13   14   15   20

◯   ◯   ◯   ◯

10. Which number sentence is a doubles fact?

$3 + 3 = 6$ $4 + 5 = 9$

◯   ◯

$3 + 6 = 9$ $7 + 1 = 8$

◯   ◯

11. Anna and Kayla each have 5 cherries. Carla has 7 cherries. How many cherries do they have in all?

_____ cherries

12. Jada has 3 cats. Talia has the same number of cats. How many cats do they have altogether?

STOP

_____ cats

Apply Subtraction Concepts

Key Vocabulary

subtract

difference

inverse

missing addend

Explore

There are 10 bowling pins. If all of the pins are knocked down, how many pins will be left standing?

_____ bowling pins

Math Online
Take the Chapter Readiness
Quiz at macmillanmh.com.

Are You Ready for Chapter 3?

Count. Write the number.

1.
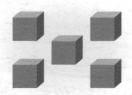
_____

2.

_____

Subtract.

3.

$4 - 3 =$ _____

4.

$6 - 3 =$ _____

5.

$3 - 2 =$ _____

6.

$9 - 7 =$ _____

Draw an X on the boxes to solve.

7.

$5 - 1 =$ _____

8.
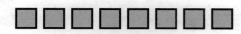

$8 - 4 =$ _____

Solve.

9. Christy put 6 marbles in a group. 2 marbles rolled away. How many marbles are left?

_____ marbles

This page checks skills needed for Chapter 3.

MATH at HOME

Dear Family,

Today my class started Chapter 3, **Apply Subtraction Concepts**. In this chapter, I will learn to use different strategies to solve subtraction problems. Here is an activity we can do and a list of books we can read together.

Love,

_____

Activity

Place up to 7 items on the table for your child to count. Take away one item. Ask how many are there now. Take away two more items. Ask how many are left.

Key Vocabulary

difference the answer to a subtraction problem

$$3 - 1 = 2 \longleftarrow \text{difference}$$

fact family addition and subtraction sentences that use the same numbers

$5 - 3 = 2$	$5 - 2 = 3$
$3 + 2 = 5$	$2 + 3 = 5$

Math Online Click on the eGlossary link at macmillanmh.com to find out more about these words. There are 13 languages.

Books to Read

Benny's Pennies
by Pat Brisson
Doubleday, 1993.

How Many Blue Birds Flew Away?
by Paul Gigianti, Jr.
Greenwillow
Publishing, 2005.

Safari Park
by Stuart J. Murphy
HarperCollins
Publishers, 2002.

Estimada familia:

Hoy mi clase comenzó el Capítulo 3, **Desarrolla conceptos de resta.** En este capítulo, aprenderé a usar diferentes estrategias para resolver problemas de resta. A continuación, hay una actividad que podemos hacer y una lista de libros que podemos leer juntos.

Cariños,

_____

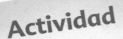

Actividad

Coloquen hasta 7 artículos sobre una mesa para que su hijo(a) los cuente. Retiren un artículo. Pregunten cuantos artículos quedan ahora. Retiren does artículos más. Pregunten cuántos artículos quedan.

Vocabulario clave

diferencia respuesta a un problema de resta

$$3 - 1 = 2 \longleftarrow \text{diferencia}$$

familia de operaciones enunciados de suma o resta que usan los mismos números

$$5 - 3 = 2 \qquad 5 - 2 = 3$$
$$3 + 2 = 5 \qquad 2 + 3 = 5$$

Math Online Visiten el enlace eGlossary en macmillanmh.com para averiguar más sobre estas palabras, las cuales se muestran en 13 idiomas.

Libros recomendados

Sumar y restar
de Dorling Kindersley Publishers
Estrella Gsp, 2006.

Restar y quitar
de Diyan Leake
Heinemann, 2006.

Name _____

Count Back to Subtract

Get Ready

Main Idea

I will use a number line to subtract.

Vocabulary

count back

subtract

difference

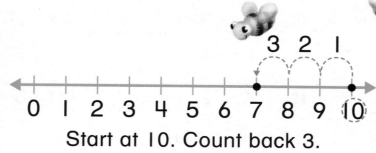

Use a number line. **Count back** to **subtract**.
You subtract to find the **difference**.
Find 10 − 3.

        3 2 1

0 1 2 3 4 5 6 7 8 9 10

Start at 10. Count back 3.

$$10 - 3 = \underline{7}$$

Check

Count back to subtract. Use the number line.

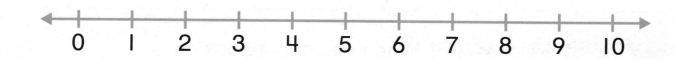

0   1   2   3   4   5   6   7   8   9   10

1.	2.	3.	4.	5.	6.
7	8	9	10	5	6
− 3	− 1	− 2	− 2	− 1	− 3
4					

7. 8 − 2 = ____   8. 7 − 1 = ____   9. 4 − 1 = ____

10. **Talk About It** Explain how you count back on a number line to find a difference.

Count back to subtract. Use the number line.

```
◄──┬───┬───┬───┬───┬───┬───┬───┬───┬───┬───┬───┬──►
   0   1   2   3   4   5   6   7   8   9   10  11  12
```

11. 3 − 2 = _____   **12.** 12 − 3 = _____   **13.** 5 − 2 = _____

14. 8 − 3 = _____   **15.** 11 − 3 = _____   **16.** 10 − 3 = _____

17. 9 − 3 = _____   **18.** 11 − 2 = _____   **19.** 3 − 1 = _____

20.　　9   **21.**　　5   **22.**　　10   **23.**　　4   **24.**　　6
　　　　− 1   　　　　− 3   　　　　− 1   　　　　− 2   　　　　− 2

25.　　3   **26.**　　4   **27.**　　8   **28.**　　7   **29.**　　6
　　　　− 2   　　　　− 3   　　　　− 1   　　　　− 2   　　　　− 1

30. 　**WRITING IN** ▶**MATH** When you count back on
a number line, what number is the difference?

_____

_____

Math at Home Activity: Say a number between 3 and 12. Have your
child subtract 1, 2, or 3. Have your child count back to find the difference.

Name _____

Subtract All and Subtract Zero

Get Ready

Main Idea

I will subtract all or zero to find the difference.

You can subtract to find the difference.
Find how many frogs are left.

Subtract all.

$5 - 5 = \underline{0}$

$\underline{0}$ frogs are left.

Subtract zero.

$5 - 0 = \underline{5}$

$\underline{5}$ frogs are left.

Check

Subtract.

1. $3 - 3 = \underline{0}$

   $3 - 0 = \underline{3}$

2. $5 - 0 = \underline{}$

   $5 - 5 = \underline{}$

3. $6 - 6 = \underline{}$

   $6 - 0 = \underline{}$

4. $\begin{array}{r} 9 \\ -0 \\ \hline \end{array}$ $\begin{array}{r} 9 \\ -9 \\ \hline \end{array}$

5. $\begin{array}{r} 4 \\ -4 \\ \hline \end{array}$ $\begin{array}{r} 4 \\ -0 \\ \hline \end{array}$

6. $\begin{array}{r} 7 \\ -7 \\ \hline \end{array}$ $\begin{array}{r} 7 \\ -0 \\ \hline \end{array}$

7. **Talk About It** Explain how you know $8 - 8 = 0$ and $8 - 0 = 8$.

Subtract. Circle the problem if the difference is zero.

8. $9 - 3 =$ _____   **9.** $8 - 1 =$ _____   **10.** $8 - 3 =$ _____

11. $4 - 4 =$ _____   **12.** $7 - 3 =$ _____   **13.** $3 - 1 =$ _____

14.
$$\begin{array}{r} 8 \\ -8 \\ \hline \end{array}$$

15.
$$\begin{array}{r} 8 \\ -2 \\ \hline \end{array}$$

16.
$$\begin{array}{r} 6 \\ -0 \\ \hline \end{array}$$

17.
$$\begin{array}{r} 5 \\ -5 \\ \hline \end{array}$$

18.
$$\begin{array}{r} 9 \\ -1 \\ \hline \end{array}$$

19.
$$\begin{array}{r} 3 \\ -2 \\ \hline \end{array}$$

20.
$$\begin{array}{r} 6 \\ -6 \\ \hline \end{array}$$

21.
$$\begin{array}{r} 7 \\ -2 \\ \hline \end{array}$$

22.
$$\begin{array}{r} 4 \\ -0 \\ \hline \end{array}$$

23.
$$\begin{array}{r} 7 \\ -7 \\ \hline \end{array}$$

24.
$$\begin{array}{r} 9 \\ -0 \\ \hline \end{array}$$

25.
$$\begin{array}{r} 8 \\ -0 \\ \hline \end{array}$$

26.
$$\begin{array}{r} 9 \\ -9 \\ \hline \end{array}$$

27.
$$\begin{array}{r} 9 \\ -2 \\ \hline \end{array}$$

28.
$$\begin{array}{r} 5 \\ -0 \\ \hline \end{array}$$

H.O.T. Problems

29. Algebra Todd had 12 beads. He lost some of them. Now he has 7 beads. Circle the subtraction sentence that shows how many beads Todd lost.

$$12 - \boxed{} = 7 \quad \text{or} \quad 12 - 7 = \boxed{}$$

30. How many beads did Todd lose?

_____ beads

Math at Home Activity: Have your child use small objects to show $5 - 5$ and $5 - 0$.

Name _____

Use Doubles to Subtract

Get Ready

Main Idea

I will use doubles facts to subtract.

You can use doubles facts to help you subtract. Find 16 − 8.

I know 8 + 8 = 16, so 16 − 8 = __8__ .

Check

Use doubles facts to help you subtract. Use cubes.

1.

9 + __9__ = 18

18 − 9 = __9__

2.

5 + ____ = 10

10 − 5 = ____

3. 6 + ____ = ____

12 − 6 = ____

4. 4 + ____ = ____

8 − 4 = ____

5. 14 − 7 = ____

6. 16 − 8 = ____

7. **Talk About It** Explain how you can use a doubles fact to subtract.

Subtract. Circle the problem if you use doubles
to subtract. Use cubes.

8. $9 - 3 =$ _____

9. $11 - 9 =$ _____

10. $5 - 5 =$ _____

11. $6 -$ _____ $= 3$

12. $7 - 3 =$ _____

13. $12 -$ _____ $= 6$

14.
$$\begin{array}{r} 16 \\ - \boxed{} \\ \hline 8 \end{array}$$

15.
$$\begin{array}{r} 7 \\ - 0 \\ \hline \end{array}$$

16.
$$\begin{array}{r} 10 \\ - \boxed{} \\ \hline 5 \end{array}$$

17.
$$\begin{array}{r} 9 \\ - 2 \\ \hline \end{array}$$

18.
$$\begin{array}{r} 6 \\ - 2 \\ \hline \end{array}$$

19.
$$\begin{array}{r} 8 \\ - 3 \\ \hline \end{array}$$

20.
$$\begin{array}{r} 14 \\ - \boxed{} \\ \hline 7 \end{array}$$

21.
$$\begin{array}{r} 7 \\ - 2 \\ \hline \end{array}$$

Data File

The Museum of Science and
Industry in Chicago is a fun
place to learn about science
and math. Hundreds of people
visit the museum each year.

22. 18 people are waiting in
line to go into the museum.
9 people go inside. How many
people are still waiting in line?
Write a number sentence to solve.

_____ − _____ = _____ people

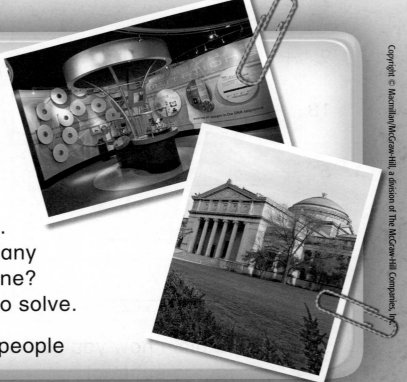

Math at Home Activity: Call out a doubles fact. Have your child name
the subtraction problem for each double.

Name _____

Problem-Solving Strategy
Guess and Check

Main Idea

I will guess and check to solve a problem.

There are 9 kittens at the animal shelter. The kittens are all orange or gray. There are 3 more gray kittens than orange kittens. How many kittens of each color are there?

Understand

What do I need to find?
Circle the question.

Plan

How will I solve the problem?

Solve

Guess and check.

_____ orange kittens, _____ gray kittens

Check

Look back.
Is my answer reasonable?

Try It

Guess and check to solve.

1. Lillian has 13 party invitations. She wants to invite 3 more girls than boys. How many girls and boys will receive invitations to Lillian's party?

_____ girls _____ boys

2. Oranges come in boxes of 4, 8, and 10. Cory bought 12 oranges. Which two boxes of oranges did he buy?

boxes of _____ and _____

Your Turn

Guess and check to solve.

3. Sunflower seeds come in packages of 7, 9, and 11. Koko wants to plant 16 seeds. Which two packages of seeds should she plant?

packages of _____ and _____

4. Bella has 18 toy cars and 3 boxes. She put the same number of cars in each box. How many cars are in each box?

_____ cars

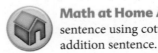

Math at Home Activity: Show your child a subtraction sentence using cotton balls. Have your child make the related addition sentence.

Name _____

Count back to subtract. Use the number line.

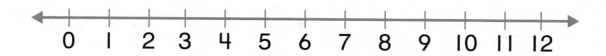

0 1 2 3 4 5 6 7 8 9 10 11 12

1. 7 − 3 = _____

2. 12 − 3 = _____

3. 11 − 2 = _____

4. 9 − 0 = _____

Subtract. Circle the problem if the difference is zero.

5.   7
      − 3
     ____

6.   3
      − 3
     ____

7.   10
      − 5
     ____

8.   8
      − 8
     ____

Subtract. Circle the problem if you use doubles to subtract.

9. 6 − 3 = _____

10. 5 − 5 = _____

11. 16 − 8 = _____

12. 8 − _____ = 4

13. Alexa had 12 pumpkins. She sold 6 of them. How many pumpkins does Alexa have now? Write a number sentence.

_____ − _____ = _____

_____ pumpkins

Find each sum.

14.		15.		16.		17.	
	1		4		6		6
	9		3		7		8
	+ 2		+ 3		+ 6		+ 4

Count back to subtract.

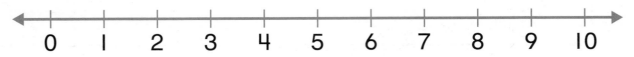

$$0 \quad 1 \quad 2 \quad 3 \quad 4 \quad 5 \quad 6 \quad 7 \quad 8 \quad 9 \quad 10$$

18. $8 - 3 = $ _____   **19.** $5 - 2 = $ _____

20. $9 - 1 = $ _____   **21.** $4 - 3 = $ _____

Add.

22. $70 + 9 = $ _____   **23.** $30 + 4 = $ _____

24. What is the value of the 2 in twenty-seven?
Circle the answer.

2   20   7   70

Compare. Write >, <, or =.

25. 83 ◯ 21   **26.** 82 ◯ 82

27. 49 ◯ 94   **28.** 61 ◯ 16

29. Ava is counting numbers. She missed a number.
Write the missing number. Name the pattern.

30, _____, 38, 42   skip counting by _____

     Formative Assessment

Name _____

Relate Addition to Subtraction

Main Idea

I will use addition facts to subtract.

Vocabulary

related facts

inverse

You can use addition facts to subtract. **Related facts** have the same three numbers.

$5 + 4 = $ _9_

$9 - 4 = $ _5_

$9 - 5 = $ _4_

Addition and subtraction are opposite or **inverse** operations.

Check

Use addition facts to subtract.

1. $6 + 7 = $ _13_ $13 - 6 = $ _7_

   $13 - 7 = $ _6_

2. $5 + 7 = $ ____ $12 - 7 = $ ____

   $12 - 5 = $ ____

3. $9 + 6 = $ ____ $15 - 6 = $ ____

   $15 - 9 = $ ____

4. $7 + 4 = $ ____ $11 - 4 = $ ____

   $11 - 7 = $ ____

5. **Talk About It** Explain how addition and subtraction are related.

Remember
Related facts use the
same three numbers.

> **Practice**

Use addition facts to subtract.

6. $\begin{array}{r} 8 \\ +9 \\ \hline \end{array}$ $\begin{array}{r} 17 \\ -8 \\ \hline \end{array}$ 7. $\begin{array}{r} 9 \\ +6 \\ \hline \end{array}$ $\begin{array}{r} 15 \\ -9 \\ \hline \end{array}$ 8. $\begin{array}{r} 9 \\ +5 \\ \hline \end{array}$ $\begin{array}{r} 14 \\ -5 \\ \hline \end{array}$ 9. $\begin{array}{r} 7 \\ +6 \\ \hline \end{array}$ $\begin{array}{r} 13 \\ -6 \\ \hline \end{array}$

10. $\begin{array}{r} 8 \\ +4 \\ \hline \end{array}$ $\begin{array}{r} 12 \\ -8 \\ \hline \end{array}$ 11. $\begin{array}{r} 8 \\ +7 \\ \hline \end{array}$ $\begin{array}{r} 15 \\ -7 \\ \hline \end{array}$ 12. $\begin{array}{r} 8 \\ +5 \\ \hline \end{array}$ $\begin{array}{r} 13 \\ -8 \\ \hline \end{array}$ 13. $\begin{array}{r} 5 \\ +7 \\ \hline \end{array}$ $\begin{array}{r} 12 \\ -5 \\ \hline \end{array}$

14. $7 + 9 =$ ____

$16 - 9 =$ ____

$16 - 7 =$ ____

15. $5 + 6 =$ ____

$11 - 6 =$ ____

$11 - 5 =$ ____

16. $6 + 8 =$ ____

$14 - 8 =$ ____

$14 - 6 =$ ____

17. $9 + 4 =$ ____

$13 - 4 =$ ____

$13 - 9 =$ ____

Problem Solving

Number Sense Circle the subtraction sentence
that you could use to check each addition sentence.

18. $9 + 4 = 13$

$13 - 1 = 12$ $13 - 4 = 9$ $10 - 4 = 6$

19. $7 + 5 = 12$

$12 - 4 = 8$ $12 - 1 = 11$ $12 - 5 = 7$

98   ninety-eight

Math at Home Activity: Ask your child to show you an addition sentence with
spoons and relate it to subtraction.

Name _____

Add or subtract.

Color answers greater than 10 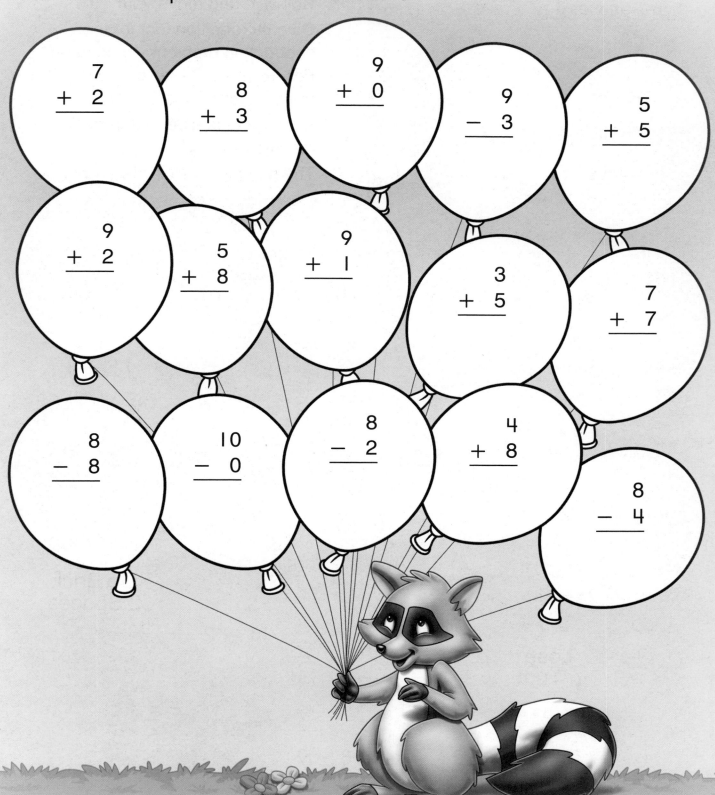 crayon .

Color answers less than 10 crayon .

Color answers equal to 10 crayon .

$$\begin{array}{r} 7 \\ + \ 2 \\ \hline \end{array}$$

$$\begin{array}{r} 8 \\ + \ 3 \\ \hline \end{array}$$

$$\begin{array}{r} 9 \\ + \ 0 \\ \hline \end{array}$$

$$\begin{array}{r} 9 \\ - \ 3 \\ \hline \end{array}$$

$$\begin{array}{r} 5 \\ + \ 5 \\ \hline \end{array}$$

$$\begin{array}{r} 9 \\ + \ 2 \\ \hline \end{array}$$

$$\begin{array}{r} 5 \\ + \ 8 \\ \hline \end{array}$$

$$\begin{array}{r} 9 \\ + \ 1 \\ \hline \end{array}$$

$$\begin{array}{r} 3 \\ + \ 5 \\ \hline \end{array}$$

$$\begin{array}{r} 7 \\ + \ 7 \\ \hline \end{array}$$

$$\begin{array}{r} 8 \\ - \ 8 \\ \hline \end{array}$$

$$\begin{array}{r} 10 \\ - \ 0 \\ \hline \end{array}$$

$$\begin{array}{r} 8 \\ - \ 2 \\ \hline \end{array}$$

$$\begin{array}{r} 4 \\ + \ 8 \\ \hline \end{array}$$

$$\begin{array}{r} 8 \\ - \ 4 \\ \hline \end{array}$$

Switcheroo
Related Facts

Play with a partner. Take Turns
- Put your ♟ on **Start**.
- Roll 🎲 and move your ♟.
- Give the addition fact for the subtraction problem you land on. For example, if the space says $7 - 6$, the addition fact is $1 + 6 = 7$.
- If your fact is a double, move forward 1 space.
- The first player to **Finish** wins!

You Will Need
- 🎲
- ♟ ♟

Start

$9 - 3$

$14 - 7$

$12 - 3$

$11 - 3$

$16 - 8$

Lose a Turn

$5 - 0$

$7 - 2$

$12 - 6$

$10 - 10$

$15 - 0$

Go Back 2 Spaces

$11 - 2$

Lose a Turn

$10 - 5$

$10 - 2$

$18 - 9$

Finish

Name _____

Missing Addends

Main Idea

I will use subtraction facts to help find missing addends.

Vocabulary

missing addend

You can use a related subtraction fact to help you find a **missing addend**.

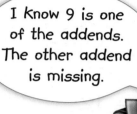

I know 9 is one of the addends. The other addend is missing.

$9 + \boxed{} = 15$

Think $15 - 9 = 6$.

So $9 + \boxed{6} = 15$

6 is the missing addend.

Check

Find the missing addend. Draw dots to help.

1.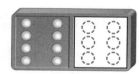

$8 + \boxed{6} = 14 \quad 14 - 8 = \boxed{6}$

2.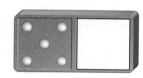

$5 + \boxed{} = 11 \quad 11 - 5 = \boxed{}$

3.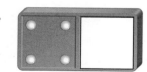

$4 + \boxed{} = 8 \quad 8 - 4 = \boxed{}$

4.

$7 + \boxed{} = 15 \quad 15 - 7 = \boxed{}$

5. **Talk About It** How do you find the missing addend in

$5 + \boxed{} = 13?$

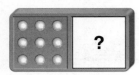
Find the missing addend.

6.   ?

$14 - 9 = \boxed{}$

$9 + \boxed{} = 14$

7. $12 - 6 = \boxed{}$

$\boxed{} + 6 = 12$

8. $8 - 7 = \boxed{}$

$7 + \boxed{} = 8$

9. $12 - 9 = \boxed{}$

$9 + \boxed{} = 12$

10. $7 - 2 = \boxed{}$

$\boxed{} + 2 = 7$

11. $15 - \boxed{} = 7$

$7 + \boxed{} = 15$

12. $\boxed{} - 7 = 7$

$7 + \boxed{} = 14$

13.
```
    9            18
+ ☐          - ☐
────         ────
 18
```

14.
```
    6            13
+ ☐          - ☐
────         ────
 13            6
```

H.O.T. Problem

15. **Algebra** There are 11 students with brown hair, red hair, and blonde hair. 5 have brown hair. 4 have red hair. How many have blonde hair?

$5 + 4 + \boxed{} = 11$

 Math at Home Activity: Ask your child to tell you the subtraction fact that will help him or her add $7 + \boxed{} = 15$.

Name _____

Fact Families

Main Idea

I will use related facts to write fact families.

Vocabulary

fact family

A **fact family** is a set of related facts about three numbers. The numbers in this fact family are 12, 9, and 3.

$9 + 3 =$ __12__

$3 + 9 =$ __12__

$12 - 9 =$ __3__

$12 - 3 =$ __9__

I can use what I know about addition and subtraction to complete fact families.

Check

Complete each fact family.

1.

$7 + 9 =$ ____ $16 - 9 =$ ____

$9 + 7 =$ ____ $16 - 7 =$ ____

2.

$9 + 8 =$ ____ $17 - 9 =$ ____

____ $+$ ____ $=$ ____   ____ $-$ ____ $=$ ____

3.
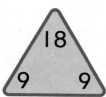

$9 + 9 =$ ____ $18 - 9 =$ ____

4. Why does Exercise 3 have only two number facts?

Copyright © Macmillan/McGraw-Hill, a division of The McGraw-Hill Companies, Inc.

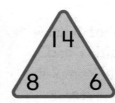
Complete each fact family.

5.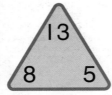

_____ + _____ = _____   _____ − _____ = _____

_____ + _____ = _____   _____ − _____ = _____

6.

_____ + _____ = _____   _____ − _____ = _____

_____ + _____ = _____   _____ − _____ = _____

7.

_____ + _____ = _____   _____ − _____ = _____

_____ + _____ = _____   _____ − _____ = _____

8.

_____ + _____ = _____   _____ − _____ = _____

_____ + _____ = _____   _____ − _____ = _____

9.

_____ + _____ = _____   _____ − _____ = _____

H.O.T. Problem

10. Algebra Find the missing number.
Write the number in the boxes.

$3 + \boxed{} = 13$ $\boxed{} - 3 = 10$

$10 + \boxed{} = 13$ $13 - \boxed{} = 3$

Math at Home Activity: Have your child name the fact family for the addition sentence $6 + 7 = 13$.

Name _____

Problem-Solving Investigation

Main Idea

I will choose a strategy to solve the problem.

Five friends came to my house. Mom put 10 bananas in a fruit basket for us. My friends and I each ate a banana. How many bananas are left?

Your Mission: Find how many bananas are left.

Understand

What do I need to find?
Circle the question.

Plan

How will I solve the problem?

Solve

One way is to write a number sentence.

_____ bananas

Check

Look back.
Is my answer reasonable?

Mixed Problem Solving

Problem-Solving Strategies
- Write a number sentence
- Find a pattern
- Act it out

Choose a strategy. Solve.

1. There were 18 rabbits at the farm. The farmer sold 9. How many rabbits were left?

_____ rabbits

2. Li always picks 2 flowers on her way home from school. If she goes to school for 5 days, how many flowers will she have by Friday?

_____ flowers

3. Two families each have 4 people in them. They all go on a picnic. Each person eats 2 hot dogs. How many hot dogs do they eat in all?

_____ hot dogs

4. Mrs. Lewis has 13 students in her reading group. 4 students are home sick. How many students are in school today?

_____ students

5. Dave adds 2 two-digit numbers. His answer is 25. One of the numbers is 10. What is the other number?

_____

Math at Home Activity: Take advantage of problem-solving opportunities during daily routines such as riding in the car, bedtime, doing laundry, putting away groceries, planning schedules, and so on.

When it was time to go back to school, Ms. Gardner said, "We are going to have a picnic on the playground before school is over this year." The students clapped and cheered!

How many students will be at the picnic? 10 + 10 = _____ students What happened when Ms. Gardner told the class about the picnic?

_____

FOLD DOWN

Problem Solving
in Language Arts

Real-World MATH

Spring is a good time for outdoor field trips. Veronica's class is going to the park.

This book belongs to

_____

After Ms. Gardner counted, the students went to play.

10 students left to go swing, but there were only 5 swings. How many students did not get to swing?

_____ students

Ms. Gardner counted all the students when they got to the park.

Usually there are 20 students in Veronica's class, but today 2 students were absent. How many students are at the park?

_____ students

Name _____

Vocabulary

Draw lines to match.

1. **missing addend**

    a. $2 + 1 = 3$ $1 + 2 = 3$
       $3 - 1 = 2$ $3 - 2 = 1$

2. **fact family**

    b. $4 - 2 = 2$

3. **subtract**

    c. $3 + \boxed{} = 7$

Concepts

Count back to subtract. Use the number line.

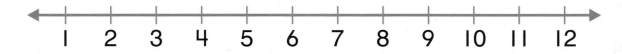

$$\begin{array}{ccccccccccccc} 1 & 2 & 3 & 4 & 5 & 6 & 7 & 8 & 9 & 10 & 11 & 12 \end{array}$$

4. $10 - 2 =$ _____

5. $9 - 3 =$ _____

Subtract. Circle the problem if the difference is zero.

6.
$$\begin{array}{r} 6 \\ -\ 6 \\ \hline \end{array}$$

7.
$$\begin{array}{r} 9 \\ -\ 9 \\ \hline \end{array}$$

8.
$$\begin{array}{r} 8 \\ -\ 3 \\ \hline \end{array}$$

9.
$$\begin{array}{r} 7 \\ -\ 1 \\ \hline \end{array}$$

Subtract. Circle the problem if you use doubles to subtract.

10. $8 - 4 =$ _____

11. $12 - 8 =$ _____

12. $10 -$ _____ $= 5$

13. $9 - 5 =$ _____

Use addition facts to subtract.

14.
$$8 \quad 14$$
$$\underline{+\,6} \quad \underline{-\,6}$$

15.
$$9 \quad 16$$
$$\underline{+\,7} \quad \underline{-\,9}$$

16.
$$9 \quad 14$$
$$\underline{+\,5} \quad \underline{-\,5}$$

---

17. Circle the related subtraction sentence.

$$8 + 5 = 13$$

$$13 - 5 = 8 \qquad 18 - 15 = 13 \qquad 12 - 5 = 7 \qquad 16 - 8 = 8$$

Find the missing addend.

18. $7 + \boxed{} = 14$

$14 - 7 = \boxed{}$

19. $5 + \boxed{} = 11$

$11 - 5 = \boxed{}$

Complete the fact family.

20.

$$\underline{\quad\quad} + \underline{\quad\quad} = \underline{\quad\quad} \qquad \underline{\quad\quad} - \underline{\quad\quad} = \underline{\quad\quad}$$

$$\underline{\quad\quad} + \underline{\quad\quad} = \underline{\quad\quad} \qquad \underline{\quad\quad} - \underline{\quad\quad} = \underline{\quad\quad}$$

Problem Solving

21. Elam drew 14 people. 9 of the people were boys. How many girls did he draw?

_____ girls

22. Jeff planted some flower seeds. 3 of the seeds grew into plants. 6 seeds did not. How many seeds did Jeff plant?

_____ seeds

Name _____

Listen as your teacher reads each problem.
Choose the correct answer.

1. Conner had 12 cents. He bought a piece of gum for 9 cents and had 3 cents left. Which fact models this situation?

3 + 9 = 12 ◯   12 − 9 = 3 ◯

9 + 3 = 12 ◯   12 − 3 = 9 ◯

2. Use the number line to count back. What is the difference?

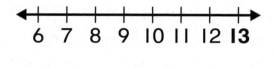

6 7 8 9 10 11 12 **13**

13 − 3 = _____

9 ◯   10 ◯   11 ◯   12 ◯

3. How many ones are in 64?

4 ◯   6 ◯   10 ◯   64 ◯

4. Which fact can help you find the missing addend?

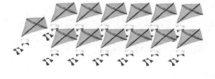

8 + ☐ = 13

13 − 8 = 5 ◯   13 + 8 = 21 ◯

13 − 6 = 7 ◯   8 − 5 = 3 ◯

5. Look at the kites. About how many kites are there?

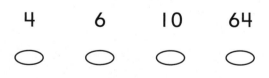

about 10 ◯   about 20 ◯

about 30 ◯   about 40 ◯

6. Which doubles fact could you use to solve?

16 − 8

7 + 7 ◯   8 + 8 ◯

9 + 9 ◯   7 + 8 ◯

Chapter 3

one hundred eleven   111

7. What is the solution to this problem?

$$9 - 1 = \underline{\hspace{1cm}}$$

7   8   9   10
○   ○   ○   ○

8. Which of these can be used to check the answer 13 − 6?

$13 + 6 = 19$ $13 - 7 = 6$
○   ○

$6 + 6 = 12$ $6 + 7 = 13$
○   ○

9. The table shows the golf balls in Penny's collection.

Penny's Golf Ball Collection	
Color	Number of Golf Balls
White	12
Green	5
Yellow	7

Which fact shows how many more white balls there are than green balls?

$12 - 7$ $12 - 5$
○   ○

$7 + 5$ $7 - 5$
○   ○

10. Which number is between 67 and 74?

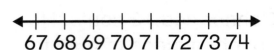

67 68 69 70 71 72 73 74

61   67   70   77
○   ○   ○   ○

11. Miguel has twelve crackers. He lets Stacey have eight. How many crackers does Miguel have left?

_____ crackers

12. Owen had 12 crayons. He let Lena borrow 6. How many crayons does Owen have left?

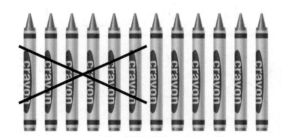

_____ crayons

Organize and Use Data

Key Vocabulary

data

picture graph

bar graph

Favorite Recess Activity	Tally	Total
Sliding	III	
Climbing	IIII	
Jumping	IIII I	

Explore

Look at the tally chart. Total the tallies. Which activity is the favorite?

_____

Math Online

Take the Chapter Readiness
Quiz at macmillanmh.com.

 Are You Ready for Chapter 4?

Circle the group that has more.

1.

2.

Use the tally chart to answer these questions.

Favorite Animal	Tally	Total
Cat	|||	3
Hamster	||||	4
Dog	卌 ||	7
Rabbit	||	2

3. Which animal has 4 tally marks?

_____

4. How many people picked cat?

_____ people

Use the picture to solve.

5. Roy walks four dogs every day.
How many brown dogs does he walk?

_____ brown dogs

6. Laura, Steve, Manuel, and Elan
play tic-tac-toe. They keep track
of their points in this chart.
Put their scores in order from
least to greatest.

Player	Tally
Laura	卌 |
Steve	卌 |||
Manuel	||
Elan	卌

_____, _____, _____, _____

This page checks skills needed for Chapter 4.

MATH at HOME

Dear Family,

Today my class started Chapter 4, **Organize and Use Data**. In this chapter, I will learn different ways to display data. Here is an activity we can do and a list of books we can read together.

Love, _____

Activity

Have your child pick five colors. Then count the number of cars of each color in a parking lot. Use tally marks to record the data.

Key Vocabulary

key tells what or how many each symbol in a graph stands for

picture graph a graph that has different pictures to show information collected

bar graph a graph that uses bars to show data

Math Online Click on the eGlossary link at macmillanmh.com to find out more about these words. There are 13 languages.

Books to Read

Five Creatures
by Emily Jenkins
Farrar, Straus and
Giroux, 2005.

How Much Is That Guinea Pig in the Window?
by Joanne Rocklin
Sagebrush Education
Resources, 1999.

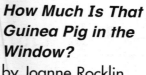

The Judge: An Untrue Tale
by Harve Zemach
Farrar, Straus and
Giroux, 1988.

Estimada familia:

Hoy mi clase comenzó el Capítulo 4, **Ordene y utilice los datos**. En este capítulo, aprenderé varias formas de presentar datos. A continuación, hay una actividad que podemos hacer y una lista de libros que podemos leer juntos.

Cariños, _____

Actividad

Pídanle a su hijo(a) que seleccione cinco colores. Luego, cuenten el número de autos de un mismo color en un estacionamiento. Usen marcas de conteo para registrar los datos. Luego, utilicen una gráfica de barras para presentar sus datos. ¿De qué color es la moda de los autos?

Vocabulario clave

clave qué o cuántos elementos representa cada símbolo

gráfica de imagen gráfica que usa imágenes para mostrar datos

gráfica de barras gráfica que usa barras para mostrar datos

Math Online Visiten el enlace eGlossary link en macmillanmh.com para averiguar más sobre estas palabras, las cuales se muestran en 13 idiomas.

Libros recomendados

Cinco criaturas
de Emily Jenkins
Farrar, Straus and Giroux, 2005.

Más mátematicas con los chocolates de m&m's
de Barbara Barbieri McGrath
Charlesbridge Publishing, 2001.

Take a Survey

Get Ready

Main Idea

I will take a survey and organize data using tally marks.

Vocabulary

survey

tally marks

data

When you take a **survey**, you ask a question. Use **tally marks** to record the answers, or data. **Data** is information.

What is your favorite type of book?

Steps for Taking a Survey

1. Write a question.

2. Ask your question.

3. Record each person's answer with a tally mark.

4. Count the number of tally marks.

Type of Book	Tally	Total
Scary	II	2
Funny	HHT III	8
Sports	HHT	5

Check

Take a survey. Ask ten students their favorite season. Use tally marks to record the data.

Use the data in the chart to answer the questions.

Favorite Season	Tally	Total
Winter		
Spring		
Summer		
Fall		

1. Which season do students like best?

_____

2. How many students like winter and fall? Write a number sentence to solve.

____ ◯ ____ = ____

3. **Talk About It** How do tally marks help you organize data?

Take a survey. Ask ten students their favorite picnic food. Use tally marks to record the data.

Picnic Food	Tally	Total
🍔		
🍗		
🌭		

Use the data in the chart to answer the questions.

4. How many children like hamburgers? _____ children

5. How many children like hot dogs? _____ children

6. What is the favorite picnic food? _____

7. How would the chart change if you added your

favorite food? _____

_____

Problem Solving

8. Using Data Students in Grade 2 took a survey for Fun Friday activities. Seven students want a picnic. Five students want to go to the zoo. Eight students want to watch a movie. Which chart shows these results? Circle the correct survey.

9. How many students were surveyed?

_____ students

Activity	Tally
Picnic	卌 I
Zoo	卌
Movie	III

Activity	Tally
Picnic	卌 II
Zoo	卌
Movie	卌 III

Math at Home Activity: Have your child think of a survey question to ask five people. Make a tally chart to show the results.

Picture Graphs

Get Ready

Main Idea

I will make picture graphs to show data.

Vocabulary

picture graph

symbol

key

You can show data with a **picture graph**. Each picture is a **symbol** for the data. The **key** tells how many each symbol stands for.

Molly took a survey about favorite pets. She made a tally chart.

Favorite Pet	Tally
🐶 Dog	||
🐱 Cat	||||

Next, Molly made a picture graph to show the data in a different way.

Favorite Pet

🐶 Dog	🐶	🐶		
🐱 Cat	🐱	🐱	🐱	🐱

Key: Each animal = 1 vote

Check

Use the tally chart to make a picture graph.

1.

Favorite Pet	Tally
🐟 Fish	卌 卌
🐦 Bird	卌	
🐹 Hamster	卌 卌 ||
🐰 Rabbit	||

Favorite Pet

🐟 Fish						
🐦 Bird						
🐹 Hamster						
🐰 Rabbit						

Key: Each animal = 2 votes

2. **Talk About It** How are picture graphs and tally charts different?

Use the tally chart to make a picture graph.

3.

Favorite Pizza Topping	Tally
Pepperoni	ⵊⵊⵊ I
Sausage	I
Cheese	ⵊⵊⵊ
Vegetables	II
Ham	ⵊⵊⵊ II

Favorite Pizza Topping

Pepperoni						
Sausage						
Cheese						
Vegetables						
Ham						

Key: Each picture = I

4.

Going to School	Tally	Total
Bus	IIII	4
Walk	ⵊⵊⵊ ⵊⵊⵊ	
Bike	II	
Car	IIII	

Going to School

Bus				
Walk				
Bike				
Car				

Key: Each picture = 2

Problem Solving

5. Using Data Look at the picture graph. 9 students voted for math. Use this information to create a key.

Key: Each picture = _____ votes

Favorite Subject

	Math	✏	✏	✏	
	Reading	📕			
	Gym	👟	👟	👟	👟

6. Use the picture graph to complete the tally chart.

7. How many students picked Gym?

_____ students

Favorite Subject	Tally
Math	
Reading	
Gym	

Math at Home Activity: Ask your child to make a picture graph of the number of shoes and socks in his or her bedroom.

Name _____

Analyze Picture Graphs

Main Idea

I will draw
conclusions
and answer
questions
based on
picture
graphs.

Think
What can we learn
from this graph?

You can get a lot of
information from
picture graphs.

Favorite Vegetable

Peas							
Corn							
Broccoli							
Red Peppers							

Key: Each vegetable = 1 vote

Check

Use the picture graph to answer the questions.

1. How many kinds of vegetables are there? _____ kinds

2. How many people chose peas or red peppers? _____ people

3. How many more people chose corn than broccoli? _____ people

4. Which vegetable had the least votes? _____

5. How many people were surveyed in all? _____ people

6. How will the graph change if you add
   another choice?

   _____

7. **Talk About It** Who could use this information?

Use the picture graph to answer the questions.

Instruments We Play

🎺 Trumpet	🎺	🎺	🎺					
🥁 Drums	🥁	🥁	🥁	🥁				
🎸 Guitar	🎸	🎸	🎸	🎸	🎸			
🎻 Violin	🎻	🎻						

Key: Each picture = 2 children

Remember:
The key tells how many children each symbol stands for.

8. How many children play the trumpet? _____ children

9. Which instrument is played by 10 children? _____

10. If 28 children took this survey, how many children do not play the violin?

    _____ children

11. Is it possible that only 5 children took this survey? Explain your answer.

    _____

    _____

H.O.T. Problem

12. **Make It Right** For Exercise 8, Jamal wrote 3 for his answer. Tell why Jamal is wrong. Make it right.

    _____

    _____

Math at Home Activity: Ask your child to make a picture graph of family members' favorite meals.

Name _____

Problem-Solving Strategy
Make a Table

Main Idea

I will make a table to solve a problem.

The breakfast special at Darla's Diner comes with 3 pancakes. 5 friends order the breakfast special. How many pancakes will they receive in all?

Understand

What do I know? Underline what you know.
What do I need to find? Circle the question.

Plan

How will I solve the problem?

Solve

Make a table.

_____ pancakes

Check

Look back.
Is my answer reasonable?

Try It

Make a table to solve.

1. Alvin likes to practice basketball in his driveway. He shoots 20 baskets every day. How many days will it take him to shoot 100 baskets?

_____ days

---

2. Desiree has 4 pairs of socks in her drawer. How many socks are there in all?

_____ socks

Your Turn

Make a table to solve.

3. Mr. Minnick needs to deliver 60 boxes. His car can hold 10 boxes at a time. How many trips will he need to make in order to deliver all 60 boxes?

_____ trips

---

4. Juice boxes come in packs of 4 at Sam's Grocery. Mrs. Perez needs 20 juice boxes in all. How many packs should she buy?

_____ packs

 Math at Home Activity: Have your child make a table to show the number of eggs in 3 cartons.

Name _____

Use the tally charts to make picture graphs.
Then answer the questions.

1.

Favorite Toy	Tally
Balls	HHT II
Skates	HHT
Stuffed animals	IIII

Favorite Toy

⚽ Balls							
Skates							
Stuffed animals							

Key: Each picture = 1

2. How many more students chose skates than stuffed animals? Write a number sentence to solve.

_____ ◯ _____ = _____ students

3.

Favorite Juice	Tally
Apple	HHT III
Orange	HHT I
Grape	II

Favorite Juice

🍎 Apple						
🍊 Orange						
🍇 Grape						

Key: Each picture = 2

4. How many students took the survey?

_____ students

5. How many students like orange juice or apple juice?

_____ students

6. How many votes does each picture stand for?

_____ votes

Find each sum.

7.   2   0
       + 0   + 2
       ___   ___

8.   3   9
       + 9   + 3
       ___   ___

9.   5   2
       + 2   + 5
       ___   ___

Use the number line to solve.

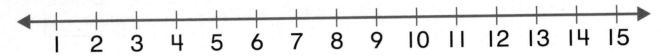

10. 8 + 3 = _____   **11.** 6 + 1 = _____   **12.** 9 + 2 = _____

Add. Use doubles facts.

13. 7 + 8 = _____   **14.** 6 + 5 = _____

15. 8 + 9 = _____   **16.** 4 + 5 = _____

Use addition facts to subtract.

17.   4   13
        + 9   − 9
        ___   ___

18.   9   15
        + 6   − 6
        ___   ___

19.   8   12
        + 4   − 4
        ___   ___

20. A tricycle has 3 wheels. How many wheels are there on 4 tricycles? Identify, describe, and extend the pattern.

This pattern _____

_____

Tricycles	Wheels
1	3
2	
3	
4	

Formative Assessment

Name _____

Bar Graphs

Main Idea

I will make a bar graph to show data.

Vocabulary

bar graph

A **bar graph** uses bars to show data. To make a bar graph, color one box for each vote. Bar graphs can look different.

One Way

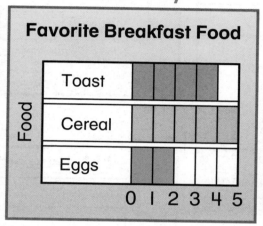

Favorite Breakfast Food

Another Way

Favorite Breakfast Food

Check

Use the tally chart to make a bar graph.

1.

Favorite Breakfast Food	Tally
Oatmeal	|||
Bagel	||||
Fruit	||
Bacon		
Muffin	ΗΗ

Favorite Breakfast Food

Food						
Oatmeal						
Bagel						
Fruit						
Bacon						
Muffin						
	0	1	2	3	4	5

2. **Talk About It** How are bar graphs different from picture graphs?

Complete the tally chart. Use the tally chart to make a bar graph.

3.

Color of Shirt	Tally	Total
Red	IIII	
Blue	HHT I	
Black	II	
Green	HHT	
White	III	

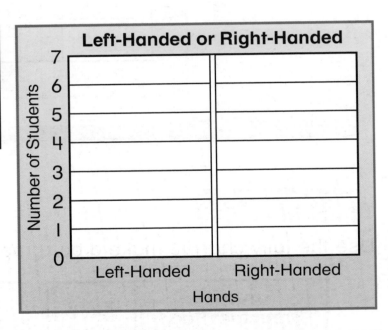

Color of Shirt

Colors: Red, Blue, Black, Green, White

0　1　2　3　4　5　6
Number of Students

4.

Left-Handed or Right-Handed	Tally	Total
Left-Handed	IIII	
Right-Handed	HHT I	

Remember
Color in 1 box
for each
tally mark.

Left-Handed or Right-Handed

Number of Students
7
6
5
4
3
2
1
0

Left-Handed　Right-Handed
Hands

5. **WRITING IN ▶MATH** Why might someone want to show data in a bar graph instead of a tally chart?

_____

_____

_____

Math at Home Activity: Ask your child to explain how he or she made one of the bar graphs on this page.

Name _____

Analyze Bar Graphs

Main Idea

I will draw conclusions and answer questions based on bar graphs.

Think
What can we learn from this graph?

Favorite Ice Cream Flavors

Number of Votes

Chocolate Vanilla Strawberry Mint
Flavors

I surveyed my classmates about favorite ice cream flavors.

Check

Use the bar graph to complete the sentences.

1. The flavor with the least votes is _____.

2. Chocolate received 2 more votes than _____.

3. Eleven students voted for _____ or _____.

4. The boy surveyed _____ classmates.

5. *Talk About It* How could this graph help a teacher plan a class party?

Use the bar graph to complete the sentences.

6. Five students have _____ hair.

7. Four students have _____ hair.

8. An equal number of students have red

hair and _____ hair.

9. _____ students were surveyed.

10. How would this graph change if 20 students took the survey?

_____

Hair Color

Hair Color	0	1	2	3	4	5
Brown						
Black						
Blonde						
Red						

Number of Students

Data File

There are different horse shows at the Kentucky State Fair. Judges vote on the horses in each show. The horse with the most votes wins the show.

11. Which horse got 6 votes?

_____

12. Which two horses got the same number of votes?

_____ and

_____

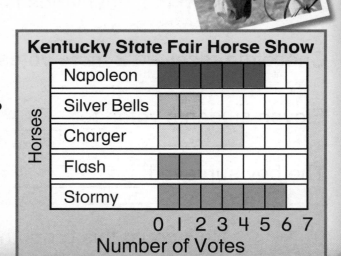

Kentucky State Fair Horse Show

Horses	0	1	2	3	4	5	6	7
Napoleon								
Silver Bells								
Charger								
Flash								
Stormy								

Number of Votes

Math at Home Activity: Ask your child to explain how to read one of the bar graphs on this page.

Name _____

Favorite Weather	Tally	Total
❄ Snow		
☀ Sun		
🌧 Rain		

Ask 8 of your classmates about their favorite weather. Make tally marks to show their answers.

Answer the questions.

1. How many of your classmates like sunny days best?

    _____ classmates

2. How many of your classmates chose snow or rain?

    _____ classmates

3. What kind of weather do the greatest number of your classmates like? _____

4. What kind of weather do the least number of your classmates like? _____

5. What types of weather have the same number of tally marks? _____

6. What is your favorite weather? _____

Spring Sports
Bar Graph

Play with three people. Take turns.
- Each player picks a crayon.
- Place the 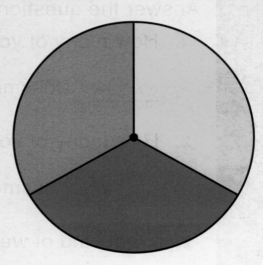 over the color wheel and spin the dial.
- If it lands on your color, shade one of the boxes in your row.
- The first runner to reach Finish wins!

You Will Need

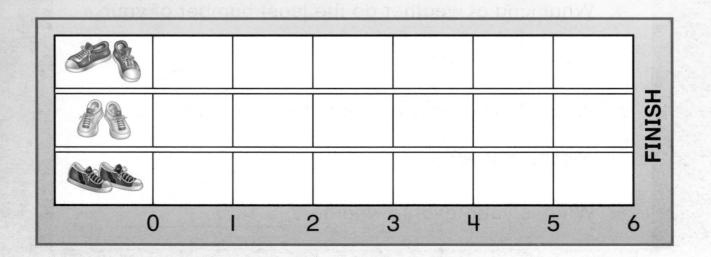

Name _____

Describe Events

Get Ready

Main Idea

I will describe events as more likely or less likely to occur.

Vocabulary

more likely

less likely

Sometimes you can tell if an event is **more likely** or **less likely** to happen.

James picks one crayon without looking. How likely is it that James will get a ⬅️▬▬▬ instead of a ⬅️▬▬?

There are more ⬅️▬▬▬ than ⬅️▬▬. James is more likely to pick a ⬅️▬▬▬.

1. James picks one crayon out of a bag.
2. He records the color on the tally chart.
3. Then he puts the crayon back in the bag. James does this 10 times.

Color	Tally
Red	ⴼꓲꓲ
Green	ꓲꓲꓲ

✓ Check

Tell if the event is more likely or less likely to happen. Then follow the steps 10 times to complete the tally chart.

Steps
1. Pick a cube.
2. Record the color in the tally chart.
3. Return the cube to the bag.

1. 4 🔲 and 2 ⬛ are in a bag.

   You are _____ to pick 🔲 instead of ⬛. Circle.

   more likely   less likely

2. Place 4 🔲 and 2 ⬛ in a bag.

Color	Tally
Green	
Purple	

3. **Talk About It** Do the results from your tally chart match your answer in Exercise 1? Explain.

Tell if the event is more likely or less likely to happen. Then follow the steps 10 times to complete the tally chart.

Steps
1. Pick a cube.
2. Record the color in the tally chart.
3. Return the cube to the bag.

4. 2 ▪ and 6 ▫ are in a bag.

You are _____ to pick ▪ instead of ▫. Circle.

more likely   less likely

5. Place 2 ▪ and 6 ▫ in a bag.

Color	Tally
Red	
Yellow	

6. 5 ▫ and 4 ▫ are in a bag.

You are _____ to pick ▫ instead of ▫. Circle.

more likely   less likely

7. Place 5 ▫ and 4 ▫ in a bag.

Color	Tally
Orange	
Yellow	

Problem Solving

8. Logical Reasoning Teresa put 5  and 5  in a bag. Is Teresa more likely to pick ▪ or more likely to pick ▪?

Explain. _____

_____

_____

_____

Math at Home Activity: Have your child put 2 red pens and 4 blue pens in a shopping bag. Ask your child which one is likely to be picked first.

Name _____

Problem-Solving Investigation

Main Idea

I will choose a strategy to solve a problem.

The pizza shop has three pizza specials. The choices are cheese, pepperoni, or ham with one of these: onions, green peppers, or olives. How many different pizzas could I order?

Your Mission:
Find how many different pizzas Maria could order.

Understand

What do I know? Underline what you know.
What do I need to find? Circle the question.

Plan

How will I solve the problem?

Solve

One way is to make a list.

_____ different pizzas

Check

Look back.
Is my answer reasonable?

Mixed Problem Solving

Problem-Solving Strategies

- Make a list
- Draw a picture
- Find a pattern

Choose a strategy. Solve.

1. My teacher says she wants all eyes looking at her. There are 24 students in my class. Each person has two eyes. How many eyes should be looking at the teacher?

_____ eyes

2. Karen has a lemonade stand. She charges 5 cents for each cup of lemonade. Karen sells 6 cups. How much money does she make?

_____ cents

3. Jeb, Ellen, and Jin are lining up to get a drink. How many different ways could they stand in line?

_____ different ways

4. Each child has 3 pennies to throw in a fountain. There are 6 children. How many pennies are there in all?

_____ pennies

Math at Home Activity: Have your child make a list to find out how many ways there are to order 4 different-colored crayons.

Use the chart. Make a bar graph to show this week's weather.

Days	Weather
Monday	 🌧
Tuesday	 ☁
Wednesday	 ☀
Thursday	 🌧
Friday	 ☀

Weather

Rainy						
Sunny						
Cloudy						
	0	1	2	3	4	5

FOLD DOWN

Problem Solving in Science

Real-World MATH

Tamika loves the weather. She likes rain and thunder. She likes snow and cold, too. Most of all, Tamika likes warm sunny days. She has been keeping track of the weather for five days in a row.

This book belongs to

_____

On Monday, the weather was rainy. On Tuesday, it was cloudy.

Days	Weather
Monday	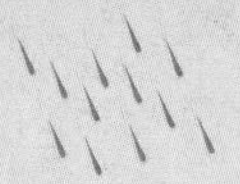
Tuesday	

How many days were sunny?

_____ days

On Wednesday, the weather was sunny, and on Thursday, it rained.

Days	Weather
Wednesday	
Thursday	

How many days so far this week have been rainy?

_____ days

Name _____

Vocabulary

Draw lines to match.

1. **data**

2. **key**

a. helps you read a graph

b. information

Concepts

Kyle's classmates voted on their favorite zoo animals.
Use the tally chart to make the picture graph.

3.

Favorite Zoo Animals	Tally
Giraffe	HHT I
Monkey	HHT III
Elephant	IIII

Favorite Zoo Animals

Giraffe								
Monkey								
Elephant								

Key: Each picture = 2 votes

Use the picture graph to answer the questions.

4. How many students like monkeys or elephants?

_____ students

5. How many students were surveyed?

_____ students

6. How many more students picked monkeys than giraffes?

_____ students

The graph shows how many students have been to the zoo. Use the tally chart to make the bar graph.

7.

Have you been to the zoo?	Tally
Yes	~~HHT~~ ~~HHT~~
No	II

Have you been to the zoo?

Yes										
No										

0 1 2 3 4 5 6 7 8 9 10
Number of Students

Use the bar graph to complete the sentences.

8. _____ students have been to the zoo.

9. _____ more students have been to the zoo than students who have not been to the zoo.

Tell if the event is more likely or less likely to happen.

10. 6 ⬛ and 3 ⬜ are in a bag. You are _____ to pick ⬛ instead of ⬜. Circle.

more likely   less likely

11. 4 ⬛ and 5 ⬛ are in a bag. You are _____ to pick ⬛ instead of ⬛. Circle.

more likely   less likely

Problem Solving

12. There are 4 giraffes at the zoo. Each giraffe has 4 legs. How many legs are there altogether?

_____ legs

Name _____

Listen as your teacher reads each problem.
Choose the correct answer.

1. Look at the graph. It shows how many goals each player scored this year. How many more goals did Carmen score than Julia?

Goals Scored

Carmen	
Vito	
Julia	

0 1 2 3 4 5 6 7 8
Number of Goals

2 ⬭   3 ⬭   4 ⬭   7 ⬭

2. Look at the tally chart. How many of Ben's classmates have just one pet?

Number of Pets	Tally
0	卌 |||
1	卌	
2			
3			

8 ⬭   7 ⬭   6 ⬭   2 ⬭

3. Look at the graph. It shows children's favorite kinds of fruit. How many of the children voted for oranges?

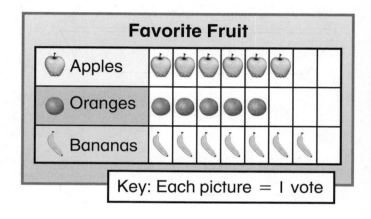

Favorite Fruit

Key: Each picture = 1 vote

4 ⬭   5 ⬭   6 ⬭   7 ⬭

4. Look at the bar graph. How much money did Fred spend in May?

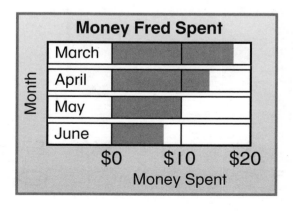

Money Fred Spent

$0 $10 $20
Money Spent

$5 ⬭ $10 ⬭ $15 ⬭ $20 ⬭

5. Look at the stickers in the drawer. Paula picked a sticker without looking. Which sticker did Paula most likely pick?

☺ ☆ ✿ ☾
◯ ◯ ◯ ◯

7. Look at the graph. It shows the number of people at the park who like hiking, tennis, or bird watching best. How many people like hiking best?

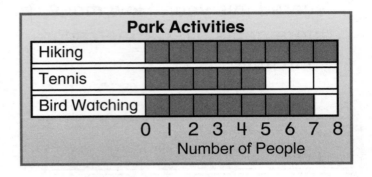

Park Activities

	0	1	2	3	4	5	6	7	8
Hiking									
Tennis									
Bird Watching									

Number of People

_____ people

6. A sandwich costs $3. A milkshake costs $2. How many dollars do the items cost in all?

$1 $5 $6 $7
◯   ◯   ◯   ◯

8. The tally chart shows how many cars from each state Tadeo saw on a trip. How many cars from Alabama did Tadeo see?

State	Tally
Virginia	|||
Alabama	ⵏⵏ ⵏⵏ	
Georgia	ⵏⵏ
Florida	ⵏⵏ |||

_____ cars

STOP

Summative Assessment

CHAPTER 5 Model Two-Digit Addition

Key Vocabulary

regroup
round

Copyright © Macmillan/McGraw-Hill, a division of The McGraw-Hill Companies, Inc.

Explore

Estimate about how many...

horses?   about _____

ears?   about _____

legs?   about _____

Math Online

Take the Chapter Readiness
Quiz at macmillanmh.com.

Are You Ready for Chapter 5?

Write each number two ways.

1. 18 ones = _____

_____ ten _____ ones

2. 26 ones = _____

_____ tens _____ ones

Add.

3. 2
      + 7
      ___

4. 3
      + 4
      ___

5. 3
      + 5
      ___

6. 1
      + 6
      ___

7. 4
      + 2
      ___

8. 9
      + 7
      ___

9. 4
      + 8
      ___

10. 8
       + 2
       ___

11. 9
       + 6
       ___

12. 6
       + 5
       ___

13. 3 + 3 + 1 = _____

14. 4 + 2 + 3 = _____

Circle the number that is closer.

15. 87 is closer to

90 or 70

16. 35 is closer to

40 or 20

Solve.

17. Jack has 5 red marbles. Tito has 3 blue
marbles. Lien has 2 green marbles. How
many marbles do they have altogether?

_____ marbles

This page checks skills needed for Chapter 5.

MATH at HOME

Dear Family,

Today my class started Chapter 5, **Model Two-Digit Addition**. In this chapter, I will learn to add two-digit numbers. Here is an activity we can do and a list of books we can read together.

Love,

_____

Activity

Have your child go on a scavenger hunt to find the number of shoes and books in your home. How many groups of 10 can your child make? How many are left over?

Key Vocabulary

regroup to take apart a number to write it in a new way

round to change the value of a number to one that is easier to work with

Math Online ▷ Click on the glossary link at <u>macmillanmh.com</u> to find out more about these words. There are 13 languages.

Books to Read

Tail Feather Fun: Counting by Tens
by Michael Dahl
Picture Window
Books, 2006.

Mall Mania
by Stuart J. Murphy
HarperCollins
Publishers, 2006.

Toasty Toes: Counting by Tens
by Michael Dahl
Picture Window
Books, 2006.

Estimada familia:

Hoy mi clase comenzó el Capítulo 5, **Haz modelos de suma con dos dígitos**. En este capítulo, aprenderé a sumar números de dos dígitos. A continuación, hay una actividad que podemos hacer y una lista de libros que podemos leer juntos.

Cariños, _____

Actividad

Pídanle a su hijo(a) que comience una búsqueda para averiguar el número de zapatos y libros que tienen en la casa. ¿Cuántos grupos de 10 puede formar su hijo(a)? ¿Cuántos sobran?

Vocabulario clave

reagrupar separar un número para escribirlo de una nueva manera

redondear cambiar el valor de en número por uno con el cual es más fácil trabajar

Math Online > Visiten el enlace eGlossary en macmillanmh.com para averiguar más sobre estas palabras, las cuales se muestran en 13 idiomas.

Libros recomendados

Come una y cuenta veinte
de Gregory Tang
Everest Publishing, 2004.

Hacer decenas: grupos de gollyluvas
de John Burstein
Weekly Reader Early Learning Library, 2006.

Name _____

Add Tens

Get Ready

Main Idea

I will use addition facts to add tens.

You can use addition facts to help you add tens.
Find 50 + 30.

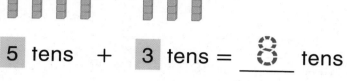

Think 5 + 3 = __8__.

__5__ tens + __3__ tens = __8__ tens

50 + 30 = __80__

Check

Add. Use 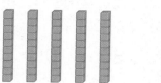 to help.

1.

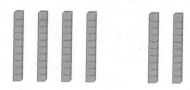

__4__ tens + __2__ tens = __6__ tens

40 + 20 = __60__

2.

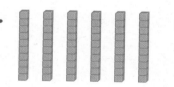

__6__ tens + __1__ ten = _____ tens

60 + 10 = _____

3. __3__ tens + __4__ tens = _____ tens

30 + 40 = _____

4. __2__ tens + __3__ tens = _____ tens

20 + 30 = _____

5. 30 + 50 = _____

6. 20 + 20 = _____

7. **Talk About It** Explain how 4 + 5 helps you find 40 + 50.

Add. Use 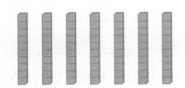 to help.

8.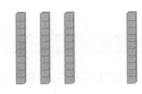

1 ten + 7 tens = _____ tens

10 + 70 = _____

9.

3 tens + 1 ten = _____ tens

30 + 10 = _____

10. 2 tens + 5 tens = _____ tens

20 + 50 = _____

11. 6 tens + 3 tens = _____ tens

60 + 30 = _____

12. 50 + 10 = _____

13. 20 + 40 = _____

14.   70
        + 10
       ———

15.   30
        + 50
       ———

16.   20
        + 20
       ———

17.   50
        + 40
       ———

18.   40
        + 30
       ———

19.   20
        + 30
       ———

20.   50
        + 20
       ———

21.   80
        + 10
       ———

22.   20
        + 70
       ———

23.   30
        + 30
       ———

Problem Solving

24. Number Sense Cora found 50 acorns on the first day of vacation. She found 10 acorns on the second day. How many acorns did Cora find in all?

_____ + _____ = _____ acorns

Math at Home Activity: Put out 10 buttons and 20 buttons. Ask your child to show an addition sentence with the buttons.

Name _____

Count On Tens and Ones

Get Ready

Main Idea

I will count on by tens and ones to find sums.

Find 26 + 3.
Count on by ones.

26 + 3 = 29

Find 26 + 30.
Count on by tens.

26 + 30 = 56

Think
Start at 26.
Count 27, 28, 29

Think
Start at 26.
Count 36, 46, 56

Check

Count on to add. Write the sum. Use  and ▮ to help.

1.

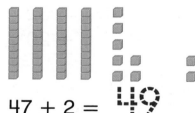

47 + 2 = 49

2.

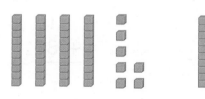

47 + 20 = _____

3.

13 + 3 = _____

4.

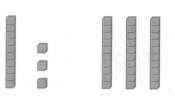

13 + 30 = _____

5. 5 + 24 = _____

6. 60 + 32 = _____

7. **Talk About It** How many tens do you count on to add 32 + 40? Explain.

Copyright © Macmillan/McGraw-Hill, a division of The McGraw-Hill Companies, Inc.

Remember
To count on by tens, keep adding 10 to the number.

Count on to add. Write the sum. Use [image] and ▪ to help.

8. $66 + 3 =$ _____

9. $12 + 70 =$ _____

10. $12 + 2 =$ _____

11. $25 + 2 =$ _____

12. $51 + 30 =$ _____

13. $25 + 10 =$ _____

14. $53 + 20 =$ _____

15. $3 + 14 =$ _____

16. $66 + 30 =$ _____

17. $51 + 3 =$ _____

18. $20 + 76 =$ _____

19. $32 + 1 =$ _____

20. $30 + 32 =$ _____

21. $3 + 32 =$ _____

22. $40 + 44 =$ _____

23.
$$\begin{array}{r} 3 \\ + 44 \\ \hline \end{array}$$

24.
$$\begin{array}{r} 10 \\ + 88 \\ \hline \end{array}$$

25.
$$\begin{array}{r} 1 \\ + 88 \\ \hline \end{array}$$

26.
$$\begin{array}{r} 32 \\ + 20 \\ \hline \end{array}$$

Problem Solving

27. Number Sense Keisha and Andy each have 25 points. Keisha scores 3 more points. How many points does Keisha have now?

Keisha has _____ points.

Andy scores 30 more points. How many points does Andy have now?

Andy has _____ points.

Math at Home Activity: Say a number between 10 and 50. Ask your child to count on by 1, 2, or 3 and then by 10, 20, or 30.

Problem-Solving Strategy
Work Backward

Main Idea

I will work backward to solve problems.

Eduardo has a baseball card collection. He gave 3 cards to Hana. Then he gave 2 cards to Patty. Eduardo now has 44 cards. How many cards did he have in the beginning?

Understand

What do I know? Underline what you know.

What do I need to find? Circle the question.

Plan

How will I solve the problem?

Solve

Work backward.
Start with the number of cards Eduardo has now. Add the cards he gave away.

Eduardo had _____ cards in the beginning.

Check

Look back.
Is my answer reasonable?

Try It

Work backward to solve.

1. During swimming lessons, the teacher passed out 23 pairs of goggles. There are 10 pairs left. How many pairs of goggles did the teacher have at the start?

_____ pairs of goggles

2. At the fair, Tamara gave 5 tickets to Jason. Then she gave 3 tickets to Shannon. Tamara has 5 tickets left. How many tickets did she have at the start?

_____ tickets

Your Turn

Work backward to solve.

3. The party store sold 15 yellow balloons and 22 orange balloons. They have 6 red balloons left. How many balloons did they have at the start?

_____ balloons

4. The art teacher handed out 17 bottles of glue. She has 9 left. How many did she have at the start?

_____ bottles of glue

Math at Home Activity: Have your child explain to you how he or she solved Exercise 4.

Name _____

Hands-On Activity

Regroup Ones as Tens

Main Idea

I will regroup to find sums.

Vocabulary

regroup

Find 27 + 5.

Step 1

Use ▭▭▭▭▭▭ and ▭ to show 27 and 5.

tens	ones

Step 2

If there are ten or more ones, **regroup** 10 ones as 1 ten.

tens	ones

Step 3

Write the number of tens and ones.

tens	ones

_3_ tens _2_ ones

27 + 5 = _32_

Check

Use WorkMat 6 and  and ▭ to add.

		Add the ones. Add the tens.	Do you regroup?	Write the sum.
1.	15 + 8	____ ten ____ ones	yes no	
2.	23 + 6	____ tens ____ ones	yes no	

3. *Talk About It* How do you know if you need to regroup?

Copyright © Macmillan/McGraw-Hill, a division of The McGraw-Hill Companies, Inc.

Remember
10 ones equal
1 ten.

Use WorkMat 6 and ▭▭▭▭▭▭▭▭ and ▭ to add.

	Add the ones. Add the tens.	Do you regroup?	Write the sum.
4. 76 + 4	_____ tens _____ ones	yes no	
5. 17 + 7	_____ ten _____ ones	yes no	
6. 32 + 6	_____ tens _____ ones	yes no	
7. 59 + 5	_____ tens _____ ones	yes no	
8. 13 + 9	_____ ten _____ ones	yes no	
9. 31 + 8	_____ tens _____ ones	yes no	
10. 25 + 6	_____ tens _____ ones	yes no	
11. 62 + 7	_____ tens _____ ones	yes no	

12. **WRITING IN ►MATH** If you add 8 to 38, will the sum be *less than* or *greater than* 40? Explain.

_____

_____

_____

Math at Home Activity: Using rocks, have your child show you 25 + 5. Ask how many tens there are in the answer.

Name _____

Add.

1. ☐4 tens + ☐2 tens = _____ tens

40 + 20 = _____

2. ☐1 ten + ☐7 tens = _____ tens

10 + 70 = _____

Count on to add. Write the sum.

3. 46 + 3 = _____

4. 1 + 30 = _____

5. 16 + 2 = _____

6. 54 + 1 = _____

7. 11 + 30 = _____

8. 45 + 40 = _____

Use WorkMat 6 and ▭▭▭▭▭▭ and ◪ to add.

	Add the ones. Add the tens.	Do you regroup?	Write the sum.
9. 33 + 5	_____ tens _____ ones	yes no	
10. 49 + 6	_____ tens _____ ones	yes no	
11. 72 + 8	_____ tens _____ ones	yes no	
12. 16 + 4	_____ ten _____ ones	yes no	
13. 29 + 2	_____ tens _____ ones	yes no	

14. Montel reads 10 pages of his favorite book each day for 7 days. How many pages does he read altogether?

_____ pages

Use data from the chart to make a bar graph.
Then answer the questions.

Amy's Family	Tally	Total
Boys	|||	
Girls	||	

Amy's Family

Boys				
Girls				

0 1 2 3 4
Number of Children

15. Write a number sentence to show the total
number of children.

_____ ◯ _____ = _____ children

16. Write a number sentence to show how many
more boys than girls.

_____ ◯ _____ = _____

Complete the fact family.

17.

_____ + _____ = _____

_____ + _____ = _____

_____ – _____ = _____

_____ – _____ = _____

18. Jordan catches lightning bugs for a week. If the
pattern continues, how many lightning bugs
will he catch on Day 5? Fill in the chart.

Day	1	2	3	4	5
Lightning bugs	2	4	6	8	

Formative Assessment

Name _____

Add One-Digit Numbers and Two-Digit Numbers

Get Ready

Main Idea

I will add one-digit and two-digit numbers.

Find 17 + 5.

Step 1
Add the ones.
7 + 5 = 12

tens	ones
☐	
1	7
+	5

Step 2
Regroup if needed.
Write how many.

tens	ones
1	
1	7
+	5
	2

Step 3
Add the tens.
1 + 1 = 2

tens	ones
1	
1	7
+	5
2	2

Check

Use WorkMat 6 and  and ◼ to add.

1.

tens	ones
1	
1	8
+	6
2	4

2.

tens	ones
☐	
4	3
+	3

3.

tens	ones
☐	
2	5
+	4

4.

☐	
1	9
+	6

5.

☐	
3	6
+	5

6.

☐	
6	8
+	4

7. **Talk About It** How did you show that you regrouped?

Use WorkMat 6 and 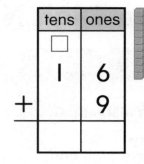 and ▢ to add.

8.

tens	ones
▢	
2	4
+	7

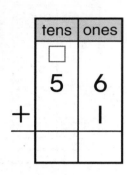

9.

tens	ones
▢	
3	5
+	5

10.

tens	ones
▢	
1	6
+	9

11.

tens	ones
▢	
5	6
+	1

12.

tens	ones
▢	
7	2
+	8

13.

tens	ones
▢	
3	8
+	8

14.

▢	
2	4
+	4

15.

▢	
4	3
+	9

16.

▢	
1	3
+	7

H.O.T. Problem

17. Make It Right Jenny says the sum of 23 and 6 is 39. Tell why Jenny is wrong. Make it right.

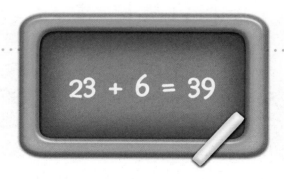

$23 + 6 = 39$

_____

_____

Math at Home Activity: Ask your child to show you how to add 14 and 8. Then ask your child to show you how to add 27 and 2.

Name _____

Add Two-Digit Numbers

Get Ready

Main Idea

I will add two-digit numbers.

Find 18 + 25.

Step 1
Add the ones.
8 + 5 = 13

tens	ones
☐	
1	8
+ 2	5

Step 2
Regroup if needed.
Write how many.

tens	ones
1	
1	8
+ 2	5
	3

Step 3
Add the tens.
1 + 1 + 2 = 4

tens	ones
1	
1	8
+ 2	5
4	3

Check

Use WorkMat 6 and  and ▢ to add.

1.

tens	ones
1	
4	7
+ 2	9
7	6

2.

tens	ones
☐	
1	2
+ 2	4

3.

tens	ones
☐	
1	5
+ 1	6

4.

☐	
8	2
+ 1	4

5.

☐	
1	5
+ 1	9

6.

☐	
3	3
+ 1	7

7. 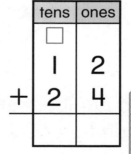 **Talk About It** What did you do first to solve Exercise 2?

> **Remember**
> Write the new ten you make above the tens place.

Use WorkMat 6 and ▭▭▭▭▭ and ▪ to add.

8.

tens	ones
☐	
1	4
+ 3	5

9.

tens	ones
☐	
3	2
+ 3	8

10.

tens	ones
☐	
1	9
+ 4	6

11.

```
  ☐
  8 | 1
+ 1 | 6
```

12.

```
  ☐
  2 | 3
+ 3 | 9
```

13.

```
  ☐
  6 | 6
+ 3 | 2
```

14.
```
   54
 + 16
```

15.
```
   35
 + 44
```

16.
```
   74
 + 16
```

Problem Solving

17. Number Sense Write a number sentence to find the total number of second graders at Summit Hall School.

Second Graders at Summit Hall School	
Ms. Smith's Class	27
Mr. Patel's Class	26

____ ◯ ____ = ____

Math at Home Activity: Take two 2-digit numbers from your phone number and have your child add them. Example: 555–1234; 12 + 34 = 46.

Name _____

Find each sum.

1. 37
  + 22
  ____

2. 44
  + 18
  ____

3. 71
  + 12
  ____

4. 36
  + 45
  ____

5. 29
  + 14
  ____

6. 28
  + 5
  ____

7. 89
  + 5
  ____

8. 16
  + 74
  ____

9. 48
  + 27
  ____

10. 66
   + 16
   ____

11. 35
   + 35
   ____

12. 44
   + 8
   ____

Pick Your Path

Add

You Will Need

- paper and pencil
-

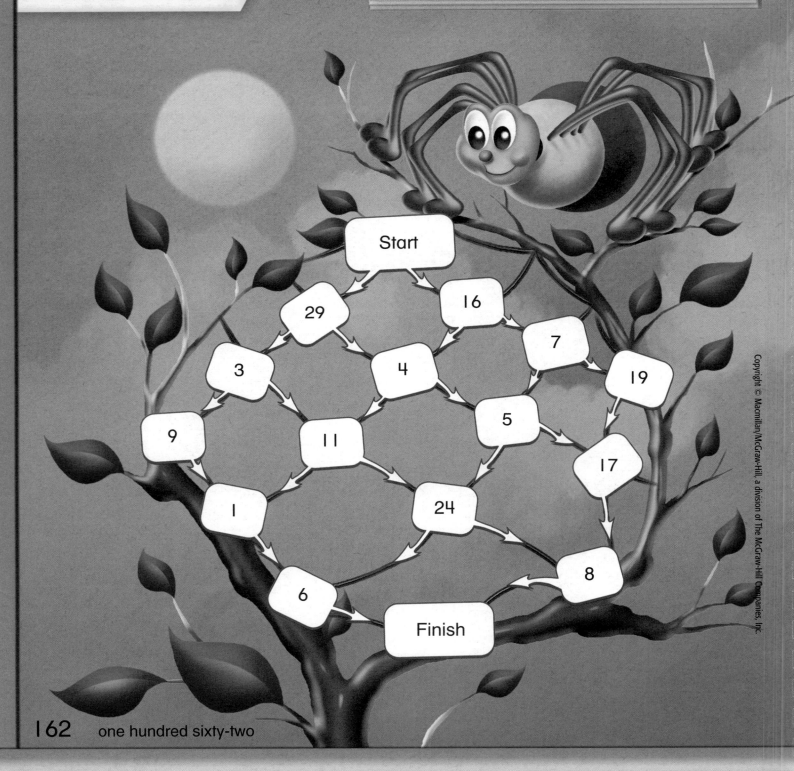

Name _____

Estimate Sums

I think I have about 30 marbles.

Get Ready

Main Idea

I will estimate the sum.

Vocabulary

round

When you do not need an exact answer, you can estimate. Estimate 14 + 19.

Step 1 Round each addend to the nearest 10.

14 is closer to 10. Round down.

10　11　12　13　14　15　16　17　18　19　20

Step 2 Add the tens to estimate the sum.

19 is closer to 20. Round up.

14	rounds to ⟹	10
+ 19	rounds to ⟹	+ 20
		30

So, 14 + 19 is about 30.

Check

Round each addend to the nearest ten. Estimate the sum.

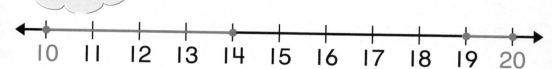

20 21 22 23 24 25 26 27 28 29 30 31 32 33 34 35 36 37 38 39 40

1. 　21 ⟶
　　+ 26 ⟶ + _____

2. 　　25
　　+ 28　+ _____

3. 　　33
　　+ 38　+ _____

4. **Talk About It** How do you estimate sums?

Round each addend to the nearest ten.
Estimate the sum.

> **Remember**
> 1, 2, 3, and 4 round down
> to the nearest ten. 5, 6,
> 7, 8, and 9 round up to
> the nearest ten.

```
  +---+---+---+---+---+---+---+---+---+---+---+---+---+---+---+---+---+---+---+---+
 30  31  32  33  34  35  36  37  38  39  40  41  42  43  44  45  46  47  48  49  50
```

5.   31
       + 47   + ___

6.   43
       + 38   + ___

7.   45
       + 38   + ___

8.   34
       + 49   + ___

9.   31
       + 32   + ___

10.   36
        + 31   + ___

11.   43
        + 30   + ___

12.   50
        + 33   + ___

13.   43
        + 33   + ___

Problem Solving

14. Thinking Math Pablo and Andrea are
shopping for building blocks. They want to know
about how much it will cost to buy both sets of
blocks. Estimate the price of both block sets.

Building Blocks	
I large set	$47
I small set	$29

about $ _____

Math at Home Activity: Ask your child to explain how to estimate
the sum of 27 and 34.

Name _____

Add Three Two-Digit Numbers

Main Idea

I will add three two-digit numbers.

I have 36 tokens.

I have 14 tokens.

I have 24 tokens. Let's add them together.

Find 36 + 14 + 24.

One Way:
Look for a ten.

```
  3 ⑥
  1 4      6 + 4 = 10
+ 2 ④
─────
  7 4      10 + 4 = 14
```

Another Way:
Look for a double.

```
  3 6
  1 ④      4 + 4 = 8
+ 2 ④
─────
  7 4      8 + 6 = 14
```

Check

Look for two numbers in the ones column that make a ten or a double. Circle them. Add.

1.
```
   1 4
     9
 + 3 1
 ─────
   5 4
```

2.
```
   3 2
   4 2
 + 1 6
 ─────
```

3.
```
   2 5
   3 3
 + 1 3
 ─────
```

4.
```
   4 2
     8
 + 3 6
 ─────
```

5.
```
   1 3
   3 3
 + 2 4
 ─────
```

6. **Talk About It** How is adding three two-digit numbers like adding two two-digit numbers?

Practice

Look for two numbers in the ones column that make a ten or a double. Circle them. Add.

7.
```
  25
   1
+ 15
```

8.
```
  51
  12
+ 32
```

9.
```
  31
  19
+ 20
```

10.
```
  13
  33
+ 45
```

11.
```
  16
   7
+ 36
```

12.
```
  18
  32
+ 13
```

13.
```
   2
  25
+ 42
```

14.
```
  34
  14
+ 17
```

15.
```
  71
  10
+  9
```

16.
```
  43
  17
+ 20
```

17.
```
  34
  13
+  3
```

18.
```
  34
  18
+ 26
```

19.
```
  15
  49
+ 15
```

20.
```
  32
  15
+ 38
```

21.
```
  28
  24
+ 36
```

Data File

The mockingbird is the state bird of Tennessee. Its song mocks, or copies, the calls of many other birds. One mockingbird can remember up to 30 different songs.

22. There are 15 mockingbirds in each bush. There are 3 bushes in all. Write a number sentence to show the total number of mockingbirds.

____ ◯ ____ ◯ ____ ◯ ____ mockingbirds

Math at Home Activity: Have your child explain how to add 28 + 12 + 35.

Name _____

Problem-Solving Investigation

Main Idea

I will choose a strategy to solve a problem.

Your Mission:
Find the two numbers.

I am thinking of two numbers. The numbers have a sum of 16 and a difference of 4. What are they?

Understand

What do I know?
Underline what you know.
What do I need to find?
Circle the question.

Plan

How will I solve the problem?

Solve

One way is to guess and check.

_____ and _____ are the numbers.

Check

Look back.
Is my answer reasonable?

Choose a strategy. Solve.

1. Parker paints 17 pictures. Jerry paints 2 more pictures than Parker. How many pictures does Jerry paint?

_____ pictures

2. Ruby and her friends pick up litter. Ruby and Trina collected a bag with 45 pieces. Stephanie and Angela collected the same number. How many pieces of litter did they collect altogether?

_____ pieces

3. Raul and Brad have toy car collections. They have 14 cars altogether. Raul has 2 more cars than Brad. How many toy cars does Raul have?

_____ cars

4. Miss Risner asked Diego to put away his cubes. He has 50 red cubes, 20 blue cubes, and 30 yellow cubes. How many cubes does he have in all?

_____ cubes

5. The baseball team divides into two groups for batting practice. Each group has 30 balls. How many balls do they have for practice in all?

_____ balls

Math at Home Activity: Take advantage of problem-solving opportunities during daily routines such as riding in the car, bedtime, doing laundry, putting away groceries, planning schedules, and so on.

It takes time to pack for a summer vacation.

D

What would you put in your suitcase if you were going away for a week?

_____

Where would you like to go?

_____

Problem Solving
in Science

Real-World MATH

Vacations are fun! You have to plan ahead when packing.

This book belongs to

_____

A

This girl's suitcase weighs 10 pounds more than the 50-pound limit. Write a number sentence to show how much the suitcase weighs.

_____ + _____ = _____ pounds

Look at this heavy suitcase. Find something in your room that is heavier than this suitcase. What did you find?

_____

B

C

Name _____

Vocabulary

Draw lines to match.

1. **regroup**

2. **round**

a. write a number in a new way

b. subtract

c. the number that occurs most often in a set of data

d. to change the value of a number so it is easier to work with

Concepts

Count on to add. Write the sum.

3. $27 + 3 =$ _____

4. $2 + 62 =$ _____

5. $82 + 3 =$ _____

6. $59 + 1 =$ _____

Add.

7. 6 tens + 3 tens = _____ tens

$60 + 30 =$ _____

8. 4 tens + 4 tens = _____ tens

$40 + 40 =$ _____

Find each sum.

9.
$$\begin{array}{r} 38 \\ + 6 \\ \hline \end{array}$$

10.
$$\begin{array}{r} 84 \\ + 2 \\ \hline \end{array}$$

11.
$$\begin{array}{r} 25 \\ + 5 \\ \hline \end{array}$$

12.
$$\begin{array}{r} 56 \\ + 7 \\ \hline \end{array}$$

13.
$$\begin{array}{r} 46 \\ + 7 \\ \hline \end{array}$$

14.
$$\begin{array}{r} 16 \\ + 4 \\ \hline \end{array}$$

15.
$$\begin{array}{r} 66 \\ + 5 \\ \hline \end{array}$$

16.
$$\begin{array}{r} 72 \\ + 8 \\ \hline \end{array}$$

Find each sum.

17.	18.	19.	20.
18 + 36	55 + 11	23 + 49	29 + 8

Round each addend to the nearest ten.
Estimate the sum.

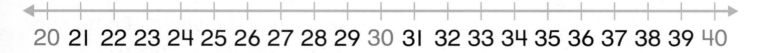

20 21 22 23 24 25 26 27 28 29 30 31 32 33 34 35 36 37 38 39 40

21.	22.
22 + 37 + ___	28 + 34 + ___

Look for two numbers in the ones column that make
a ten or a double. Circle them. Add.

23.	24.	25.	26.
42 15 + 12	22 18 + 30	11 55 + 31	16 43 + 24

Problem Solving

27. Vicky has 14 colored pencils. Kai brings
12 colored pencils. Juanita brings 20 colored
pencils. How many colored pencils do they
have altogether?

_____ colored pencils

28. Emilio has 58 stickers. Mick has 33 stickers.
How many stickers do they have altogether?

_____ stickers

Summative Assessment

Name _____

Listen as your teacher reads each problem.
Choose the correct answer.

1. Look at the graph. How many shells did Nate and Pat collect altogether?

Shells Collected

Nate	🐚	🐚	🐚	🐚	🐚	
Pat	🐚	🐚	🐚	🐚		

Key: Each 🐚 = 2

18   20   22   24
○   ○   ○   ○

2. Which addition fact will help you to add 50 + 30?

$$50 + 30$$

5 + 3   9 + 2
○   ○

7 + 2   5 + 30
○   ○

3. Use the number line to count on. What is the sum?

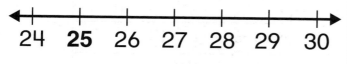

24   **25**   26   27   28   29   30

$$25 + 4 = \_\_\_$$

26   28   29   30
○   ○   ○   ○

4. There were 32 buses at school on Monday. There were 29 buses on Tuesday. How many buses were there in all on Monday and Tuesday?

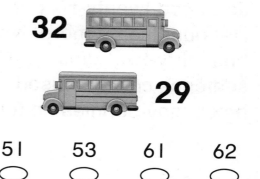

32

29

51   53   61   62
○   ○   ○   ○

5. How can you find the total number of tens in 61 and 35?

tens	ones

1 + 5   6 + 3
○   ○

6 + 5   1 + 3
○   ○

6. How many tens and ones are in 15 + 12?

$$15 + 12 = \_\_\_ \text{ tens} \_\_\_ \text{ ones}$$

1 ten 7 ones   2 tens 5 ones
○   ○

2 ten 7 ones   2 tens 8 ones
○   ○

7. What is the solution to this problem?

$$50 + 20 = \underline{\hspace{1cm}}$$

30   60   70   80
○   ○   ○   ○

8. John had twenty-six pennies. He found some more. Now he has thirty-two. Which number sentence could be used to find how many pennies he found?

$26 - \square = 32$ $26 + 32 = \square$
○   ○

$32 - 10 = \square$ $26 + \square = 32$
○   ○

9. Look at the addition problem in the box. Which other problem has the same answer?

$$26 + 14 + 19 = 59$$

○ $19 + 14 + 26 = \square$
○ $59 + 14 + 19 = \square$
○ $26 + 19 + 12 = \square$
○ $14 + 19 + 20 = \square$

10. Which sign makes the number sentence true?

$$34 + 28 \;\square\; 62$$

−   +   =   >
○   ○   ○   ○

11. The chart shows the boxes of juice sold on three days. What is the total number of juice boxes sold?

Day	Tally	Total
Friday	TITI TITI TITI TITI I	21
Saturday	TITI TITI TITI TITI TITI	25
Sunday	TITI TITI TITI TITI III	23

_____ juice boxes

12. The tally chart shows how many shells Jason found on three days. How many shells did Jason find on Friday and Sunday?

Day	Number of Shells
Friday	TITI TITI III
Saturday	TITI III
Sunday	TITI II

_____ shells

Summative Assessment

Chapter 6 Model Two-Digit Subtraction

Review Vocabulary
- regroup
- estimate
- round

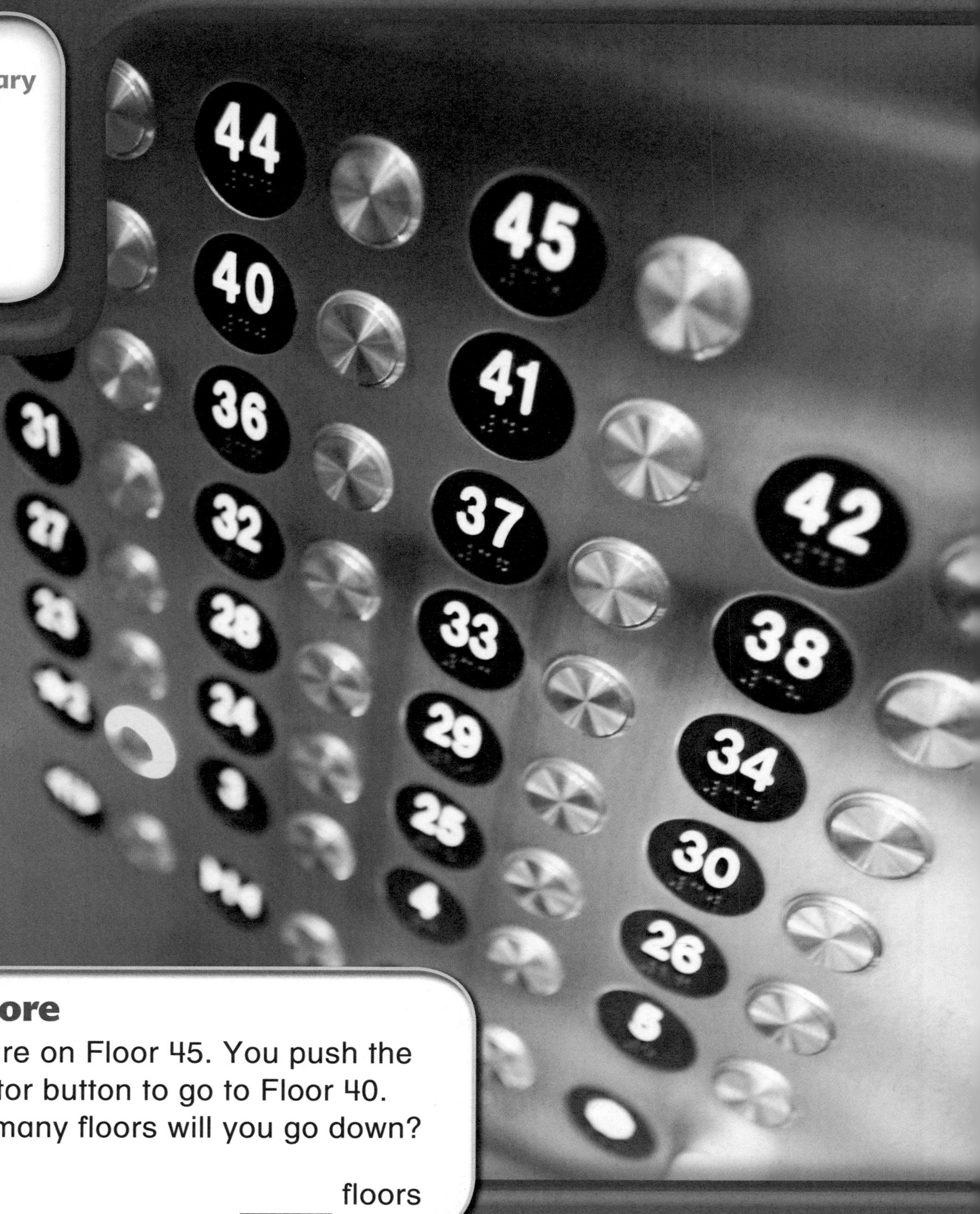

Explore

You are on Floor 45. You push the elevator button to go to Floor 40. How many floors will you go down?

_____ floors

Name _____

Math Online
Take the Chapter Readiness
Quiz at macmillanmh.com.

Are You Ready for Chapter 6?

Write how many.

1. How many tens are in 30? _____

2. How many tens are in 70? _____

3. How many tens are in 90? _____

Use the number line. Round to the nearest ten.

10   15   20   25   30   35   40

4. 26 _____   5. 18 _____

6. 13 _____   7. 31 _____

8. 37 _____   9. 22 _____

Subtract.

10. 4 − 3 = _____   11. 5 − 3 = _____

12. 9 − 6 = _____   13. 8 − 2 = _____

14. 7 − 2 = _____   15. 6 − 5 = _____

Solve.

16. Maggie has 10 crackers in her lunch.
    If Lamont eats 4 of Maggie's crackers,
    how many crackers are left?

    _____ ◯ _____ ◯ _____ crackers

This page checks skills needed for Chapter 6.

Dear Family,

Today my class started Chapter 6, **Model Two-Digit Subtraction**. In this chapter, I will learn to subtract two-digit numbers. Here is an activity we can do and a list of books we can read together.

Love, _____

Activity

Count out 50 beans, paper clips, or buttons. Have your child close his or her eyes while you take some of them away. Count the items left on the table and figure out how many are missing.

Review Vocabulary

regroup to take apart a number to write it in a new way

estimate to find a number close to an exact amount

 **Math Online** Click on the eGlossary link at macmillanmh.com to find out more about these words. There are 13 languages.

Books to Read

Math for All Seasons
by Gregory Tang
Scholastic Press,
2002.

The Relatives Came
by Cynthia Rylant
Simon & Schuster
Children's Publishing,
1985.

Shark Swimathon
by Stuart J. Murphy
HarperCollins
Publishers, 2001.

Estimada familia:

Hoy mi clase comenzó el Capítulo 6, **Modelo Resta con dos dígitos.** En este capítulo, aprenderé a restar números de dos dígitos. A continuación, hay una actividad que podemos hacer y una lista de libros que podemos leer juntos.

Cariños, _____

Actividad

Cuenten 50 frijoles, clips o botones Pídanle a su hijo(a) que cierre los ojos mientras ustedes retiran algunos. Cuenten los objetos que quedan en la mesa y averigüen cuántos faltan.

Repaso de vocabulario

reagrupar separar un número para escribirlo de una nueva manera

estimar hallar un número cercano a una cantidad exacta

Math Online Visiten el enlace eGlossary en macmillanmh.com para averiguar más sobre estas palabras, las cuales se muestran en 13 idiomas.

Libros recomendados

¿Cuanto dinero?
de Hollie J. Endres
Capstone Press, 2006.

Un, dos, tres el año se fue
de Gregory Tang
Everest Publishing, 2004.

Name _____

Subtract Tens

Get Ready

Main Idea

I will use subtraction facts to subtract tens.

You can use subtraction facts to help you subtract tens.

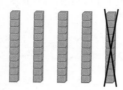

5 − 1 = 4 helps me know 50 − 10 = 40.

5 tens − 1 ten = __4__ tens

5 0 − 1 0 = __40__

Check

Subtract. Use a subtraction fact and 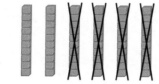 to help.

1.

6 tens − 4 tens = _____ tens

6 0 − 4 0 = _____

2.

4 tens − 2 tens = _____ tens

4 0 − 2 0 = _____

3. 3 tens − 1 ten = _____ tens

30 − 10 = _____

4. 5 tens − 2 tens = _____ tens

50 − 20 = _____

5. 80 − 40 = _____

6. 70 − 30 = _____

7. **Talk About It** How does 9 − 6 help you find 90 − 60?

Subtract. Use a subtraction fact and 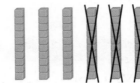 to help.

8.

4 tens − 3 tens = _____ ten

40 − 30 = _____

9.

6 tens − 3 tens = _____ tens

60 − 30 = _____

10. 5 tens − 3 tens = _____ tens

50 − 30 = _____

11. 6 tens − 1 ten = _____ tens

60 − 10 = _____

12. 60 − 40 = _____

13. 70 − 40 = _____

14. 20 − 10	**15.** 80 − 30	**16.** 70 − 30	**17.** 40 − 20	**18.** 70 − 60
19. 90 − 50	**20.** 50 − 20	**21.** 80 − 20	**22.** 90 − 60	**23.** 60 − 20

Problem Solving

24. Number Sense Nia bought 60 markers. 20 of them are blue markers. The rest are green markers. How many green markers did Nia buy?

_____ green markers

Math at Home Activity: Place 6 dimes (tens) on a table. Cover 4 dimes (tens). Ask your child how many dimes are left. 60¢ − 40¢ = 20¢

Name _____

Count Back by Tens and Ones

Get Ready

Main Idea

I will count back by tens and ones to find the difference.

Find 57 − 3.
Count back by ones.

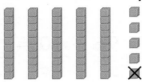

57 − 3 = __54__

Think
Start at 57.
56, 55, 54

Find 57 − 30.
Count back by tens.

57 − 30 = __27__

Think
Start at 57.
47, 37, 27

Check

Count back to subtract. Write the difference.
Use ▭▭▭ and ▭ to help.

1.

   37 − 2 = __35__

   Think
   36, 35

2.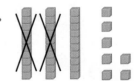

   37 − 20 = _____

3.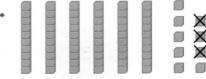

   69 − 3 = _____

4.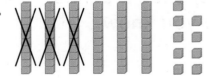

   69 − 30 = _____

5. **Talk About It** Explain how you solved Exercises 3 and 4.

Practice

Count back to subtract. Write the difference.
Use ⬛⬛⬛⬛⬛⬛ and ◻ to help.

6. $24 - 2 =$ _____

7. $24 - 20 =$ _____

8. $79 - 3 =$ _____

9. $79 - 30 =$ _____

10. $96 - 1 =$ _____

11. $96 - 10 =$ _____

12. $54 - 3 =$ _____

13. $54 - 30 =$ _____

14. $34 - 1 =$ _____

15. $34 - 10 =$ _____

16.
$$\begin{array}{r} 61 \\ -\ 1 \\ \hline \end{array}$$

17.
$$\begin{array}{r} 6 \\ -\ 2 \\ \hline \end{array}$$

18.
$$\begin{array}{r} 68 \\ -\ 3 \\ \hline \end{array}$$

19.
$$\begin{array}{r} 78 \\ -\ 1 \\ \hline \end{array}$$

20.
$$\begin{array}{r} 87 \\ -\ 30 \\ \hline \end{array}$$

21.
$$\begin{array}{r} 45 \\ -\ 20 \\ \hline \end{array}$$

22.
$$\begin{array}{r} 87 \\ -\ 3 \\ \hline \end{array}$$

23.
$$\begin{array}{r} 66 \\ -\ 1 \\ \hline \end{array}$$

H.O.T. Problem

24. **Thinking Math** Gavin and Angelo each have
5 dimes and 7 pennies. Gavin spends 3 pennies.
Angelo spends 2 dimes. Who has more money?
Tell how you know.

_____

_____

_____

Math at Home Activity: Ask your child to count back by tens to answer this problem: $53 - 20$.

Name _____

Regroup Tens as Ones

Main Idea

I will regroup to find differences.

Review Vocabulary

regroup

Find 24 − 8.

Step 1	**Step 2**	**Step 3**
Use ▭▭▭ and ▫ to show 24.	Subtract the ones. There are not enough ones to subtract. Regroup.	Subtract 8 ones.

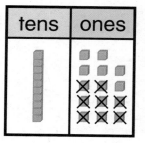

Step 1	**Step 2**	**Step 3**
2 tens 4 ones	1 ten 14 ones	1 ten 6 ones
		24 − 8 = __16__

Check

Use WorkMat 6 and ▭▭▭▭ and ▫ to subtract.

	Subtract the ones. Do you need to regroup?	Write the difference.
1. 31 − 4	no yes	31 − 4 = _____
2. 27 − 5	no yes	27 − 5 = _____

3. **Talk About It** How do you know when you need to regroup? Explain.

Remember
If there are not enough ones to subtract, regroup 1 ten as 10 ones.

Use WorkMat 6 and ▭▭▭▭ and ▪ to subtract.

	Subtract the ones. Do you need to regroup?	Write the difference.
4. $42 - 6$	no yes	$42 - 6 = $ _____
5. $21 - 2$	no yes	$21 - 2 = $ _____
6. $35 - 9$	no yes	$35 - 9 = $ _____
7. $40 - 8$	no yes	$40 - 8 = $ _____
8. $56 - 5$	no yes	$56 - 5 = $ _____
9. $22 - 6$	no yes	$22 - 6 = $ _____
10. $33 - 4$	no yes	$33 - 4 = $ _____
11. $43 - 3$	no yes	$43 - 3 = $ _____

12. **WRITING IN ►MATH** If you subtract 5 from 23, will the difference be less than 20 or greater than 20? Explain.

_____

_____

Math at Home Activity: Have your child use straws to show you how to subtract 7 from 25.

Problem-Solving Strategy
Write a Number Sentence

Main Idea

I will write a number sentence to solve problems.

There are 10 bees on a flower. 4 bees fly away. How many bees are now on the flower?

Understand

What do I know? Underline what you know.
What do I need to find? Circle the question.

Plan

How will I solve the problem?

Solve

Write a number sentence.

_____ ◯ _____ = _____ bees

Check

Look back.
Is my answer reasonable?

Try It

Write a number sentence to solve.

1. There are 15 ants in an ant hill. 3 ants
   leave. How many ants are there now?

_____ ◯ _____ ◯ _____ ants

2. A squirrel found 12 acorns.
   Then he found 5 more. How many
   acorns does he have now?

_____ ◯ _____ ◯ _____ acorns

Your Turn

Write a number sentence to solve.

3. There are 18 lions in the yard at the zoo.
   8 lions ran into the lion house.
   How many lions are left in the yard?

_____ ◯ _____ ◯ _____ lions

4. There are 22 parrots in a tree. 3 more join
   them. How many total parrots are there?

_____ ◯ _____ ◯ _____ parrots

5. Bill planted 12 daisies. His sister, Sarah,
   planted 9 daisies. How many more daisies
   did Bill plant than Sarah?

_____ ◯ _____ ◯ _____ daisies

Math at Home Activity: Ask your child to subtract 52 − 17.
Then have your child show you how to check the answer.

Name _____

Subtract.

1. 50 − 40 = _____   **2.** 80 − 20 = _____   **3.** 60 − 10 = _____

Count back to subtract. Write the difference.

4. 88 − 30 = _____   **5.** 75 − 3 = _____   **6.** 28 − 2 = _____

7.   82
        − 20
        _____

8.   49
        − 1
        _____

9.   54
        − 40
        _____

Use WorkMat 6 and ⬛⬛⬛⬛⬛⬛⬛ and ⬛ to subtract.

	Subtract the ones. Do you need to regroup?	Write the difference.
10. 25 − 7	no yes	25 − 7 = _____
11. 33 − 2	no yes	33 − 2 = _____
12. 62 − 4	no yes	62 − 4 = _____

13. Ivan had 54 crayons. He let Paul borrow 30 of them. How many crayons does Ivan have left?

_____ crayons

14. There are 15 students in line. Five students go back to their desks. How many students are in line now?

_____ students

Subtract. Circle the problems in which you used
doubles to subtract.

15. $9 - 4 =$ _____

16. $12 -$ _____ $= 6$

17. $14 - 7 =$ _____

18. $18 -$ _____ $= 9$

Find each missing number.

19. $16 - 8 =$ _____

$8 +$ _____ $= 16$

20. $14 - 5 =$ _____

$5 +$ _____ $= 14$

Solve.

21.
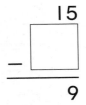
$\begin{array}{r} 15 \\ - \square \\ \hline 9 \end{array}$

22.
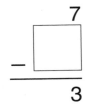
$\begin{array}{r} 7 \\ - \square \\ \hline 3 \end{array}$

23.
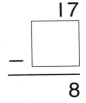
$\begin{array}{r} 17 \\ - \square \\ \hline 8 \end{array}$

Circle your estimate.

24.

?   **10 pickles**

about 10   about 20   about 30

25.

?   **10 marbles**

about 10   about 20   about 80

Round each addend to the nearest ten.
Estimate the sum.

26. $53 + 26$

26. $31 + 39$

_____ $+$ _____ $=$ _____

27. $53 + 26$

_____ $+$ _____ $=$ _____

Formative Assessment

Name _____

Subtract One-Digit Numbers from Two-Digit Numbers

Get Ready

Main Idea

I will model subtracting one-digit numbers from two-digit numbers.

Find 34 − 6.

Step 1
Show 34.
Can you subtract 6 ones?

tens	ones
3	4
	6

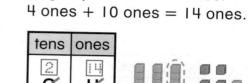

Step 2
Regroup 1 ten as 10 ones.
4 ones + 10 ones = 14 ones.

tens	ones
2̸3	14̸4
	6

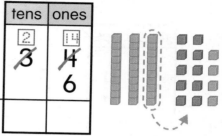

Step 3
Subtract the ones.

tens	ones
2̸3	14̸4
	6
	8

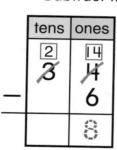 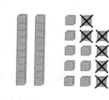

Step 4
Then subtract the tens.

tens	ones
2̸3	14̸4
	6
2	8

34 − 6 = __28__

Check

Use WorkMat 6 and  and ⬛ to subtract.

1.
tens	ones
2	3
	5

2.
tens	ones
5	8
	4

3.
tens	ones
2	6
	9

4. **Talk About It** How do you regroup 1 ten?

Use WorkMat 6 and ▭▭▭▭▭ and ▪. Subtract.

5.

tens	ones
☐ 2	☐ 7
−	8

6.

tens	ones
☐ 3	☐ 2
−	7

7.

tens	ones
☐ 3	☐ 6
−	5

8.

tens	ones
☐ 3	☐ 4
−	7

9.

tens	ones
☐ 7	☐ 4
−	3

10.

tens	ones
☐ 5	☐ 4
−	4

Problem Solving

11. Critical Thinking You have 4 tens and 6 ones on a mat. What is the greatest number of ones you can subtract **without** having to regroup? How do you know?

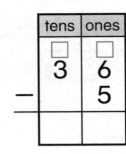

tens	ones

_____

_____

_____

_____

Math at Home Activity: Ask your child to show you how to subtract 8 from 27.

Name _____

Subtract Two-Digit Numbers

Get Ready

Main Idea

I will model subtracting two-digit numbers.

Find 52 − 17.

Step 1
Show 52.
Can you subtract 7 ones?

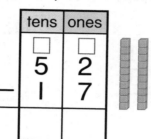

tens	ones
□ 5	□ 2
− 1	7

Step 2
Regroup 1 ten as 10 ones.
2 ones + 10 ones = 12 ones.

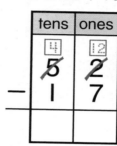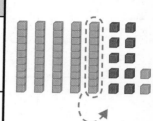

tens	ones
4 5̸	12 2̸
− 1	7

Step 3
Subtract the ones.

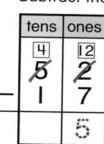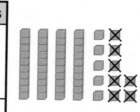

tens	ones
4 5̸	12 2̸
− 1	7
	5

Step 4
Then subtract the tens.

tens	ones
4 5̸	12 2̸
− 1	7
3	5

52 − 17 = __35__

Check

Use WorkMat 6 and and ▪ to subtract.

1.

tens	ones
□ 3̸	□ 5̸
− 1	7

2.

tens	ones
□ 4	□ 7
− 2	4

3.

tens	ones
□ 4	□ 1
− 1	6

4. **Talk About It** How is subtracting 41 − 16 different than subtracting 41 − 6?

Subtract.

5.

tens	ones
□	□
5	0
− 2	4

6.

tens	ones
□	□
8	2
− 3	7

7.

tens	ones
□	□
3	7
− 2	9

8.

```
  □ │ □
  2 │ 6
− 1 │ 9
────┼────
```

9.

```
  □ │ □
  7 │ 4
− 1 │ 8
────┼────
```

10.

```
  □ │ □
  4 │ 6
− 2 │ 3
────┼────
```

11.   87
        − 72

12.   34
        − 26

13.   47
        − 36

Problem Solving

14. Using Data Write a question for the answer.

Shells Collected								
Olivia								
Luis								
Kendra								

0   2   4   6   8   10   12   14   16

If the answer is Olivia, the question could be...

_____ ?

If the answer is 24, the question could be...

_____ ?

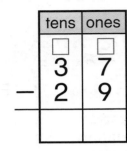 **Math at Home Activity:** Ask your child to show you how to subtract 24 from 41.

Name _____

Find each difference. **Remember** to regroup
if you do not have enough ones.

1. $\begin{array}{r} 15 \\ -\ 5 \\ \hline \end{array}$

2. $\begin{array}{r} 59 \\ -\ 53 \\ \hline \end{array}$

3. $\begin{array}{r} 73 \\ -\ 70 \\ \hline \end{array}$

4. $\begin{array}{r} 17 \\ -\ 8 \\ \hline \end{array}$

5. $\begin{array}{r} 51 \\ -\ 39 \\ \hline \end{array}$

6. $\begin{array}{r} 32 \\ -\ 25 \\ \hline \end{array}$

7. $\begin{array}{r} 61 \\ -\ 59 \\ \hline \end{array}$

8. $\begin{array}{r} 62 \\ -\ 47 \\ \hline \end{array}$

9. $\begin{array}{r} 72 \\ -\ 58 \\ \hline \end{array}$

10. $\begin{array}{r} 32 \\ -\ 19 \\ \hline \end{array}$

11. $\begin{array}{r} 80 \\ -\ 79 \\ \hline \end{array}$

12. $\begin{array}{r} 63 \\ -\ 59 \\ \hline \end{array}$

13. $\begin{array}{r} 42 \\ -\ 37 \\ \hline \end{array}$

14. $\begin{array}{r} 27 \\ -\ 19 \\ \hline \end{array}$

15. $\begin{array}{r} 70 \\ -\ 57 \\ \hline \end{array}$

16. $\begin{array}{r} 23 \\ -\ 13 \\ \hline \end{array}$

Game Time

Hit the Target
Subtract

Play with a partner. Take turns.

- Put each ♟ on the number 25.
- Roll the 🎲.
- Find the difference between the number you are on and the number on the cube.
- Take 1 ⬤ if you need to regroup.
- Move to the next circle.
- Keep playing until both players reach the center of the target.
- The player with the most counters wins.

You Will Need

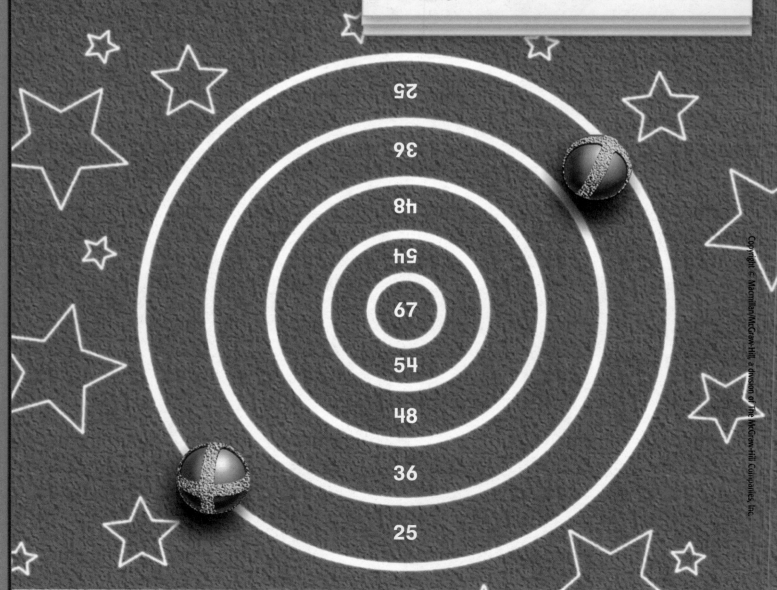

25
36
48
54
67
54
48
36
25

Name _____

Check Subtraction

Get Ready

Main Idea

I will use addition to check subtraction.

Check 25 − 10 = 15.

Subtract		**Check by Adding**	
25 − 10 15	Add these numbers to check.	15 + 10 25	If this is the number you subtracted from, your answer is correct.

To check the answer to a subtraction problem, add back the number you subtracted. The sum should match the number you subtracted from.

25 − 10 = 15
15 + 10 = 25

Check

Subtract. Check by adding.

1. 36   16
       − 20 + 20
        16   36

2. 52
       − 12   + ____
       ____

3. 21
       − 3   + ____
       ____

4. 32
       − 14   + ____
       ____

5. 85
       − 48   + ____
       ____

6. 42
       − 17   + ____
       ____

7. **Talk About It** Why does addition work as a check for subtraction?

Subtract. Check by adding.

8. 57
    − 30   + _____

9. 60
    − 10   + _____

10. 42
    − 5   + _____

11. 75
    − 41   + _____

12. 67
    − 32   + _____

13. 41
    − 26   + _____

14. 74
    − 28   + _____

15. 56
    − 28   + _____

16. 56
    − 11   + _____

17. 34
    − 9   + _____

18. 47
    − 31   + _____

Data File

New Jersey is a great place for people who enjoy sailing.

Day	People Sailing
Friday	97
Saturday	38

19. How many more people went sailing on Friday than Saturday? Check your answer.

_____ people

Math at Home Activity: Ask your child to solve 23 − 16. Then have your child show you how to check the answer.

Name _____

Problem-Solving Investigation

Main Idea

I will choose a strategy to solve a problem.

I subtracted two numbers. The greater number is 14. The next number is 2 more than 9. What is the difference between the two numbers?

Your Mission:
Find the difference between the two numbers.

Understand

What do I know?
Underline what you know.
What do I need to find?
Circle the question.

Plan

How will I solve the problem?

Solve

One way is to act it out.

The difference is _____.

Check

Look back.
Is my answer reasonable?

Mixed Problem Solving

Problem-Solving Strategies

- Act it out
- Write a number sentence
- Draw a picture

Choose a strategy. Solve.

1. There are 45 lizards in the pet shop.
   Each day, 5 lizards are purchased.
   How many lizards are left after 7 days?

_____ lizards

2. Reid had 2 sets of 10 cubes. He took
   2 cubes from each set. How many cubes
   does he have left?

_____ cubes

3. Sonia went fishing with her uncle. They
   caught 23 fish. Her uncle caught 12 fish.
   How many fish did Sonia catch?

_____ fish

4. Brett's dog likes dog bones. There are
   60 dog bones in a box. Brett's dog is only
   allowed to have 2 bones a day. How many
   bones will he have left after 10 days?

_____ bones

5. Hugo and Will put their cubes together.
   They have 78 cubes. Hugo had 26 cubes.
   How many cubes did Will have?

_____ cubes

Math at Home Activity: Take advantage of problem-solving
opportunities during daily routines such as riding in the car, bedtime,
doing laundry, putting away groceries, planning schedules, and so on.

Estimate Differences

Get Ready

Main Idea

I will estimate to find the difference.

Review Vocabulary

estimate
round

You can estimate when you do not need an exact answer. Estimate 39 − 31.

Step 1 round each number to the nearest 10.

31 is closer to 30.
39 is closer to 40.

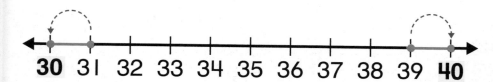

Step 2 Subtract the tens to estimate the difference.

$$39 \xrightarrow{\text{rounds to}} 40$$
$$-31 \xrightarrow{\text{rounds to}} -30$$
$$10$$

Check

Round each number to the nearest ten.
Estimate the difference.

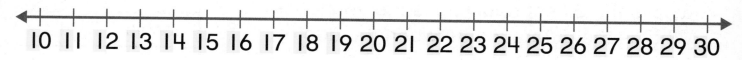

1.   31
   − 18   − _____

2.   22
   − 14   − _____

3.   45
   − 19   − _____

4. **Talk About It**   Explain how to estimate the difference of 39 and 21.

Copyright © Macmillan/McGraw-Hill, a division of The McGraw-Hill Companies, Inc.

> **Remember**
> 0, 1, 2, 3, and 4 round down. 5, 6, 7, 8, and 9 round up.

Round each number to the nearest ten.
Estimate the difference.

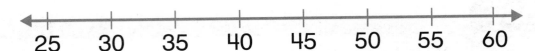

25   30   35   40   45   50   55   60

5.   38
   – 27 – _____

6.   29
   – 23 – _____

7.   36
   – 28 – _____

8.   43
   – 22 – _____

9.   58
   – 37 – _____

10.   45
   – 37 – _____

11.   51
   – 39 – _____

12.   55
   – 26 – _____

13.   42
   – 23 – _____

H.O.T. Problem

14. Explaining Math Look at the chart. Tell who is the oldest and who is the youngest. What is the difference between the age of the oldest student and the age of the youngest student?

Students' Ages	
Sophia	13
Theo	15
Madison	10
Chen	11

_____

_____

_____

Math at Home Activity: Ask your child to show you how to estimate and solve 46 – 12.

She has 23 pieces left to sew. 14 of them
are squares and the rest are triangles.
How many more triangles does she need?

_____ triangles

Look at the quilt.
The pattern tells Sharice
that she needs 2 more blue
squares. The rest should be yellow. How
many more yellow squares does she need?

_____ yellow squares

D

Problem Solving
in Social Studies

Real-World MATH

Sharice likes to quilt with her
grandmother. They are making
a quilt that tells the story of
their family.

This book belongs to

_____

A

She tells Sharice that quilts were used to help slaves escape on the Underground Railroad. Certain patterns indicated safety and direction. This one is called "Flying Geese." It gave a direction to follow.

Name a direction this quilt could give you.

_____

Their quilt shows that there are 7 people in Sharice's family.

How can you tell there are 7 people in her family?

_____

Sharice's grandmother tells her about the tradition of quilting while they work.

B

C

Name _____

Review Vocabulary

Draw lines to match.

1. **estimate**

2. **regroup**

a. to find a number close to an exact amount

b. to take apart a number

Concepts

Subtract.

3. $80 - 10 =$ ____

4. $90 - 20 =$ ____

5. $40 - 20 =$ ____

Count back to subtract. Write the difference.

6. $74 - 30 =$ ____

7. $75 - 2 =$ ____

8. $36 - 1 =$ ____

Subtract.

9. $\begin{array}{r} 23 \\ -\ 5 \\ \hline \end{array}$

10. $\begin{array}{r} 55 \\ -24 \\ \hline \end{array}$

11. $\begin{array}{r} 26 \\ -19 \\ \hline \end{array}$

12. $\begin{array}{r} 48 \\ -29 \\ \hline \end{array}$

13. $\begin{array}{r} 27 \\ -\ 8 \\ \hline \end{array}$

14. $\begin{array}{r} 32 \\ -\ 7 \\ \hline \end{array}$

15. $\begin{array}{r} 36 \\ -\ 5 \\ \hline \end{array}$

16. $\begin{array}{r} 18 \\ -\ 8 \\ \hline \end{array}$

17. $\begin{array}{r} 46 \\ -\ 5 \\ \hline \end{array}$

18. $\begin{array}{r} 30 \\ -\ 7 \\ \hline \end{array}$

19. $\begin{array}{r} 22 \\ -\ 8 \\ \hline \end{array}$

20. $\begin{array}{r} 19 \\ -\ 9 \\ \hline \end{array}$

Find each difference.

21. 45
    − 28

22. 59
    − 19

23. 74
    − 48

24. 85
    − 16

25. 65
    − 47

26. 75
    − 37

27. 43
    − 21

28. 32
    − 28

29. Peter solved this subtraction problem.
    Write the addition problem that checks
    his answer.

        57
      − 30   + _____
        27

Round each number to the nearest ten. Estimate the difference.

30. 38 − 23

_____ − _____ = _____

31. 33 − 29

_____ − _____ = _____

Problem Solving

32. There were 18 alligators around the pool at the
    zoo. 10 alligators slid into the water to swim.
    How many alligators were left around the pool?

    _____ ◯ _____ ◯ _____ alligators

33. Ana baked muffins with her mom. They baked
    24 muffins. They dropped 15 of them on the
    floor. How many muffins were left?

    _____ ◯ _____ ◯ _____ muffins

Name _____

Listen as your teacher reads each problem.
Choose the correct answer.

1. Matt sees 42 planes. King sees 9 planes. How many more planes does Matt see than King?

43   33   20   10
○   ○   ○   ○

2. How many students own blue and silver bike helmets?

Color of Helmet	Tally
Blue	⧚⧚ IIII
Silver	⧚⧚ ⧚⧚ II
Black	⧚⧚ II

14   17   19   21
○   ○   ○   ○

3. The graph shows favorite recess activities. How many like swinging the best?

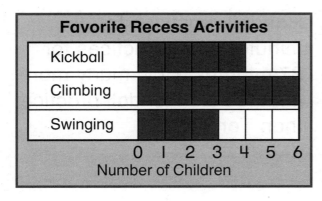

Favorite Recess Activities

Kickball

Climbing

Swinging

0 1 2 3 4 5 6
Number of Children

3   4   5   6
○   ○   ○   ○

4. What is the answer to this problem?

$$\begin{array}{r} 41 \\ -\ 28 \\ \hline \end{array}$$

13   19   23   69
○   ○   ○   ○

5. Ruben picked a flower without looking. Which flower did Ruben most likely pick?

○   ○   ○   ○

6. Mary had 50 minutes of homework. Carl's homework took 23 minutes. How many more minutes did Mary work?

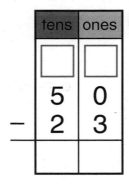

tens	ones
5	0
− 2	3

17   27   37   73
○   ○   ○   ○

7. Continue the pattern by looking at the number that goes with each shape.

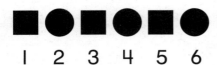

1 2 3 4 5 6

What shape would number 10 be?

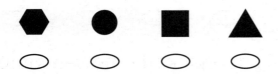

○   ○   ○   ○

---

8. Berta saw 15 birds in her yard. Mandy saw 11 birds. How many more birds did Berta see than Mandy?

3   4   5   6
○   ○   ○   ○

---

9. Which sign makes the number sentence true?

$$75 \boxed{} 6 = 69$$

+   =   <   −
○   ○   ○   ○

---

10. Look at the chart. How many cans did Pia and Kami collect?

Cans Collected	
Pia	44
Kami	38

72 cans   74 cans
○   ○

82 cans   84 cans
○   ○

---

11. Look at the chart. How many more books has Ezra read than Tia?

Reading Club	
Ezra	92 books
Tia	85 books
Mike	71 books

_____ books

---

12. Randall practices for 35 minutes. Tori practices for 27 minutes. How many more minutes did Randall practice than Tori?

_____ minutes

Summative Assessment

CHAPTER 7

Determine the Value of Money

Key Vocabulary

- cent (¢)
- half-dollar
- dollar
- dollar sign ($)
- decimal point

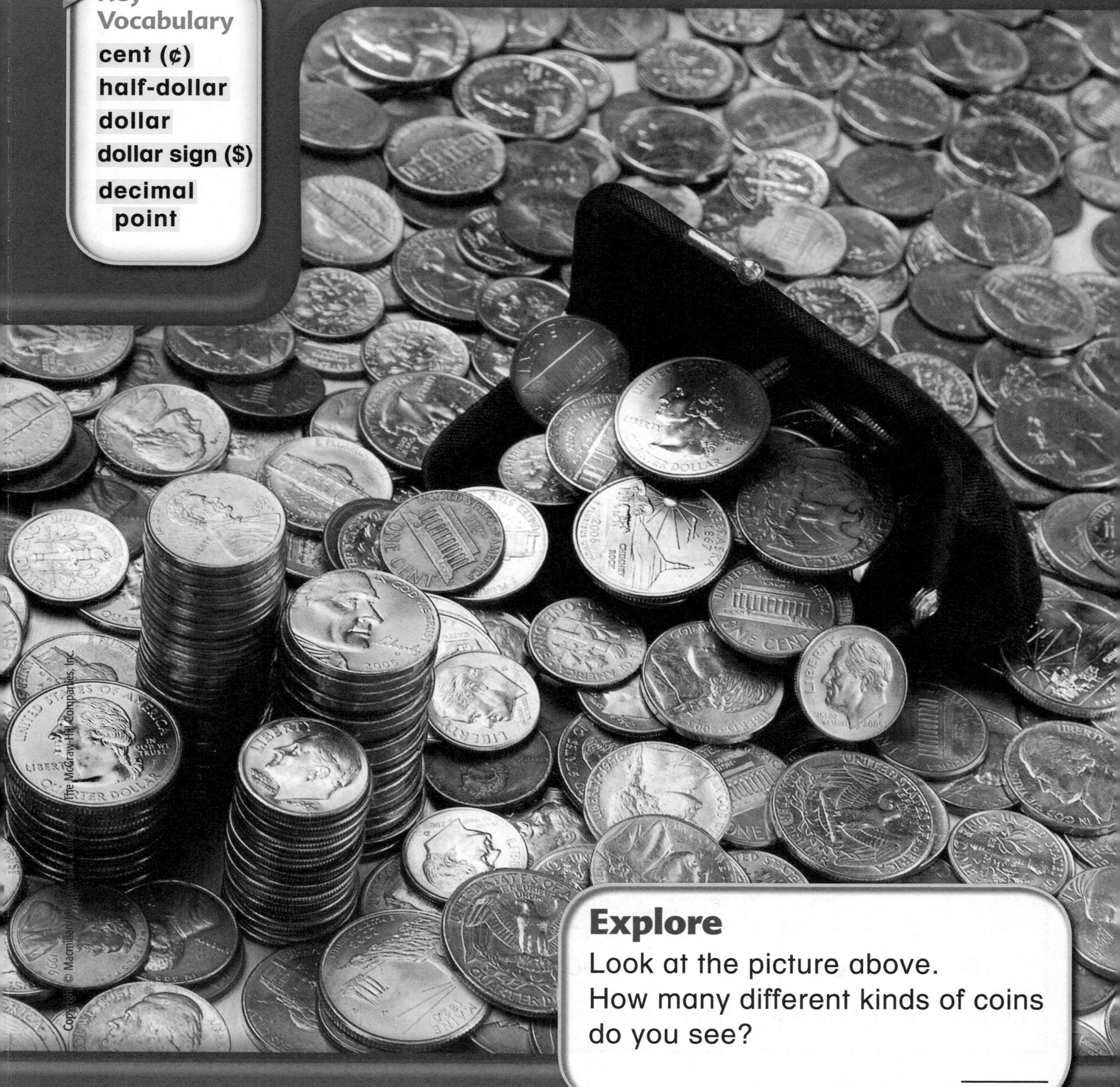

Explore

Look at the picture above.
How many different kinds of coins do you see?

______

Name _____

Are You Ready for Chapter 7?

Match each coin to its value.

1. penny   10 cents

2. nickel   5 cents

3. dime   1 cent

Add or subtract.

4.   23   5.   45   6.   76   7.   82   8.   56
    + 14   − 31   + 15   − 47   + 24
    ____   ____   ____   ____   ____

Skip count by 5s.

9. 5, 10, 15, _____, 25, _____, 35, _____, _____

---

10. Ellie earns 10 pennies every day this week.
    How many pennies will Ellie have on
    Thursday, Friday, and Saturday?

Sunday	Monday	Tuesday	Wednesday	Thursday	Friday	Saturday
10	20	30	40	_____	_____	_____
pennies	pennies	pennies	pennies	pennies	pennies	pennies

This page checks skills needed for Chapter 7.

Dear Family,

Today my class started Chapter 7, **Determine the Value of Money**. In this chapter, I will learn to add money, subtract money, and make change. Here is an activity we can do and a list of books we can read together.

Love,

_____

Activity

Look at different coins with your child and discuss ways to identify them. Have your child tell one thing about each coin. For example, have them tell you its name, value, or what is on the coin.

Key Vocabulary

half-dollar worth 50 cents or 50¢

dollar  worth 100 cents, 100¢, or $1.00

decimal point a point used in a number

$1.25

dollars · decimal point · cents

Math Online Click on the eGlossary link at macmillanmh.com to find out more about these words. There are 13 languages.

Books to Read

The Go-Around Dollar
by Barbara Johnston Adams
Simon & Schuster Children's Publishing, 1992.

Sluggers' Car Wash
by Stuart J. Murphy
HarperCollins Publishers, 2002.

Pigs Will Be Pigs
by Amy Axelrod
Aladdin, 1997.

Estimada familia,

Hoy mi clase comenzó el Capítulo 7, **Determina el valor del dinero**. En este capítulo, aprenderé a sumar y a restar dinero y a dar vuelto. A continuación, hay una actividad que podemos hacer y una lista de libros que podemos leer juntos.

Cariños,

_____

Actividad

Observen diferentes monedas con su hijo(a) y hablen sobre las formas de identificarlas. Pida a su hijo(a) que le diga algo sobre cada moneda. Por ejemplo, el nombre, el valor o qué muestra la moneda.

Vocabulario clave

medio dólar vale 50 centavos ó 50¢

dólar  vale 100 centavos 100¢ ó $1.00

punto decimal punto que se usa en un número

$1.25

dólares | punto decimal | centavos

Math Online Visiten el enlace eGlossary en macmillanmh.com para averiguar más sobre estas palabras, las cuales se muestran en 13 idiomas.

Libros recomendados

Tod el apretado
de Daphne Skinner
The Kane Press, 2005.

Haciendo dinero
de Abby Jackson
Capstone Press, 2006.

Pennies, Nickels, and Dimes

Get Ready

Main Idea

I will skip count and count on to determine the value of a collection of coins.

Vocabulary

dime

nickel

penny

cent ¢

Find the value of these coins. Start with the coin that has the greatest value.

dime = 10¢

Count by 10s.

10¢ 20¢

nickel = 5¢

Count on by 5s.

25¢ 30¢

penny = 1¢

Count on by 1s.

31¢ 32¢

32¢ total

Think
¢ stands for **cents**.

Check

Count to find the value of the coins.

1.

_____¢, _____¢, _____¢, _____¢, _____¢, _____¢   _____¢

2.

_____¢, _____¢, _____¢, _____¢, _____¢, _____¢   _____¢

3. Describe how the cent symbol is used to name the value of coins.

Count to find the value of the coins.

4.

_____ ¢, _____ ¢, _____ ¢, _____ ¢, _____ ¢, _____ ¢   _____ ¢ total

5.

_____ ¢, _____ ¢, _____ ¢, _____ ¢, _____ ¢, _____ ¢   _____ ¢ total

6.

_____ ¢, _____ ¢, _____ ¢, _____ ¢, _____ ¢, _____ ¢   _____ ¢ total

7.

_____ ¢, _____ ¢, _____ ¢, _____ ¢, _____ ¢, _____ ¢   _____ ¢ total

Name _____

▶ **Practice** with Technology

Use 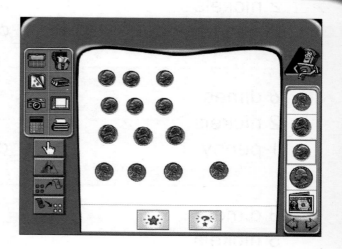 (Level 1) to count money.

- Choose the Open workmat.

- Stamp out 6 dimes.

- Stamp out 3 nickels.

- Stamp out 4 pennies.

Count by 10s.	Count by 5s.	Count by 1s.
		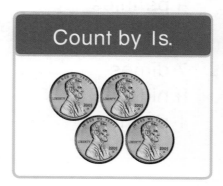

The total amount is ___79___ ¢.

Use the money button.
Stamp out each coin to find the total value.

8. 5 dimes
3 nickels
2 pennies   _____ ¢

9. 1 dime
1 nickel
5 pennies   _____ ¢

10. 4 dimes
3 nickels
4 pennies   _____ ¢

11. 3 dimes
2 nickels
6 pennies   _____ ¢

Use the ▣ (Level 1).
Stamp out each coin to find the total value.

12. 5 dimes
2 nickels
2 pennies _____¢

13. 7 dimes
3 nickels
4 pennies _____¢

14. 6 dimes
2 nickels
1 penny _____¢

15. 4 dimes
6 nickels
3 pennies _____¢

16. 3 dimes
5 nickels
4 pennies _____¢

17. 2 dimes
2 nickels
7 pennies _____¢

18. 7 dimes
4 nickels
1 penny _____¢

19. 1 dime
7 nickels
9 pennies _____¢

Problem Solving

20. Number Sense Chase has 5 dimes, and Dan
has 10 nickels. Who has more money? Explain.

_____

_____

_____

_____

Math at Home Activity: Ask your child to count a collection of
pennies, nickels, and dimes totaling less than $1.00.

Name _____

Quarters and Half-Dollars

Main Idea

I will count on to determine the value of a collection of coins.

Vocabulary

quarter

half-dollar

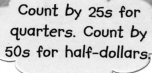

Count by 25s for quarters. Count by 50s for half-dollars.

A **quarter** is worth 25 cents.

 or

25¢

A **half-dollar** is worth 50 cents.

 or

50¢

Find the value of these coins. Start with the coin that has the greatest value.

50¢, 75¢, 80¢

80¢

Check

Count to find the value of the coins.

1.

_____ ¢, _____ ¢, _____ ¢, _____ ¢

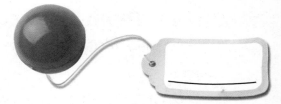

2.

_____ ¢, _____ ¢, _____ ¢, _____ ¢, _____ ¢

3. **Talk About It** Explain how you would write the value of 1 quarter, 2 dimes, and 1 nickel using the ¢ symbol.

Count to find the value of the coins.

4.

_____ ¢, _____ ¢, _____ ¢, _____ ¢, _____ ¢, _____ ¢

5.

_____ ¢, _____ ¢, _____ ¢, _____ ¢, _____ ¢

6.

_____ ¢, _____ ¢, _____ ¢, _____ ¢, _____ ¢

H.O.T. Problem

7. **Make It Right** Joey counted his money like this.

25¢, 35¢, 45¢, 55¢

Tell why Joey is wrong. Make it right.

_____

_____

Math at Home Activity: Ask your child to find the value of 1 half-dollar, 1 quarter, 1 dime, and 1 nickel.

Name _____

Count Coins

Get Ready

Main Idea

I will count on to determine the value of a collection of coins.

86¢

Find the total value of the coins. Start with the coin that has the greatest value. Is there enough money to buy the hat?

yes

no

50¢, 75¢, 85¢, 86¢

Check

Use coins. Count to find the value. Do you have enough money to buy the item? Circle *yes* or *no*.

1.

50¢, 60¢, 65¢, 66¢

68¢

yes

no

2.

_____¢, _____¢, _____¢, _____¢, _____¢

30¢

yes

no

3. **Talk About It** Why is it helpful to put coins in order by their value before you count them?

Use coins. Count to find the value.
Do you have enough money to buy the item?
Circle *yes* or *no*.

4.

_____¢, _____¢, _____¢, _____¢, _____¢

yes

no

60¢

5.

_____¢, _____¢, _____¢, _____¢, _____¢

yes

no

95¢

6.

_____¢, _____¢, _____¢, _____¢, _____¢

yes

no

68¢

Problem Solving

7. Number Sense Jewel has 1 half-dollar,
2 pennies, and 2 dimes. She wants to buy
this hat for 75¢. Does she have enough
money? Explain.

75¢

_____

_____

Math at Home Activity: Give your child a group of coins. Have your
child put the coins in order starting with the coin of greatest value.

Name _____

Problem-Solving Strategy
Act It Out

Main Idea

I will act it out to solve a problem.

Art has 1 quarter, 3 dimes, 2 nickels, and 4 pennies. Does he have enough money to buy this toy?

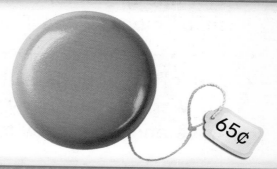

65¢

Understand

What do I know? Underline what you know.
What do I need to find? Circle the question.

Plan

How will I solve the problem?
I will use coins to act out or show how much money Art has.
I will count the total and compare it to the cost of the toy.

Solve

Act it out.

Does Art have enough money to buy the toy? _____

Check

Look back.
Is my answer reasonable?

Copyright © Macmillan/McGraw-Hill, a division of The McGraw-Hill Companies, Inc.

Try It

Act it out to solve.

1. Tina has I quarter in her piggy bank.
   Her mom gives her a nickel.
   Her dad gives her a dime. How
   much money does Tina have in all?

   _____

2. Mark has 2 quarters, I dime, and I penny.
   He wants to buy a toy truck for 55¢. Does he
   have enough money to buy the toy truck?

   _____

Your Turn

Act it out to solve.

3. Wesley has 2 quarters, 3 dimes, and 2 nickels.
   He has enough money to buy a race car.
   What is the greatest amount of money that
   the race car could cost?

   _____

4. Kim is at the toy store. She has I half-dollar
   and I quarter. What is the most Kim can pay
   for a toy?

   _____

5. Dario does not have enough money to buy this
   boat. He needs 15¢ more. How much money
   does Dario have?

   _____

Math at Home Activity: Have your child show you the coins needed to buy a toy that costs 64¢.

Name _____

Count to find the value of the coins.

1.

_____¢, _____¢, _____¢, _____¢, _____¢, _____¢   _____

2.

_____¢, _____¢, _____¢, _____¢, _____¢   _____

3.

_____¢, _____¢, _____¢, _____¢, _____¢, _____¢   _____

4.

_____¢, _____¢, _____¢, _____¢, _____¢, _____¢   _____

5. Sylvia has 2 quarters, 3 dimes, and 1 nickel.
   How much money does she have in all?

          _____

Write <, >, or =.

6. 54 ◯ 51   7. 22 ◯ 37   8. 88 ◯ 33

9. 90 ◯ 91   10. 69 ◯ 69   11. 25 ◯ 52

Write the fact family.

12.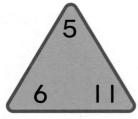

_____ + _____ = _____

_____ + _____ = _____

_____ − _____ = _____

_____ − _____ = _____

Find each sum.

13.
$$\begin{array}{r} 6 \\ 8 \\ +\ 6 \\ \hline \end{array}$$

14.
$$\begin{array}{r} 5 \\ 7 \\ +\ 4 \\ \hline \end{array}$$

15.
$$\begin{array}{r} 8 \\ 9 \\ +\ 9 \\ \hline \end{array}$$

16.
$$\begin{array}{r} 10 \\ 6 \\ +\ 3 \\ \hline \end{array}$$

Write the number.

17. 3 tens + 7 ones = _____   18. 9 tens + 1 one = _____

19. A sandwich costs $3 at the diner. Angel orders 6 sandwiches for her family. How much money do the sandwiches cost?

_____

Formative Assessment

Dollar

Hands-On Activity

Get Ready

Main Idea

I will use coins to make one dollar.

Vocabulary

dollar

dollar sign

decimal point

A **dollar** has a value of 100 cents or 100¢. When you write one dollar, use a **dollar sign** and a **decimal point**. A decimal point separates dollars from cents.

One-dollar bill
$1.00

dollar   decimal
sign   point

You can use different coins to make $1.00.

100 pennies = 100 cents	20 nickels = 100 cents	10 dimes = 100 cents	4 quarters = 100 cents	2 half dollars = 100 cents

Gin needs $1.00 to buy some pencils.
Here are the coins Gin has.

What amount of money does Gin have? __87__ ¢

Does she have enough money to buy the pencils? yes   (no)

Use these coins to make one dollar.
Write the number of coins you used.

Amount					
$1.00	1. __2__	2. _____	3. _____	4. _____	5. _____

You need exactly $1.00 to buy stickers.
Count the coins. Write the value. Circle the
combinations that equal $1.00.

6.

_____

7.

_____

8.

_____

9.

_____

10. **Talk About It** Describe how $ and ¢ are different.
How are they alike?

GO on

> ## Practice

You need exactly $1.00 to buy bottled water. Count the coins. Write the value. Circle the combinations that equal $1.00.

11.

_____

12.

_____

13.

_____

14.

_____

15.

_____

16.

_____

17.

_____

18.

_____

two hundred twenty-five **225**

You need exactly $1.00 to buy a bus ticket.
Count the coins. Write the value. Circle the
combinations that equal $1.00.

19.

_____

20.

_____

21.

_____

22.

_____

Data File

This is the North Carolina state quarter.
The quarter has a picture of the first
airplane and the words "First Flight"
because the first airplane flight took place
in North Carolina.

23. Max has 4 North Carolina state quarters.
How much money does he have?

_____

Math at Home Activity: Ask your child to show you coin
combinations that equal $1.00.

Name _____

Write the amount. Is there enough money to buy the item?
Circle *yes* or *no*.

What I Want to Buy	How Much I Have	Do I Have Enough?
1. 79¢		yes no _____
2. stickers 52¢		yes no _____
3. Coloring Book 96¢		yes no _____
4. 63¢		yes no _____

Money "Cents"
Add Coins

Play with a partner. Take turns.

○ Put your ♟ on Start.

○ Roll the 🎲 and move that number of spaces.

○ Show that amount of money.

○ If you land on $1.00, take another turn.

○ When you both get to Finish, put your coins in groups that equal $1.00.

○ Count your money. The player with more money wins.

What You Need

○ 🎲
○ paper and pencil
○ ♟ ♟
○ coins

$1.00   51¢   35¢   72¢
46¢   **START**
19¢
7¢   26¢   12¢   29¢
FINISH $1.00
37¢
33¢   74¢   58¢   4¢

Name _____

Add Money

Main Idea

I will add money.

You add money the same way you add other numbers. Just remember to write ¢ in your answer.

Find 21¢ + 18¢.

$$
\begin{array}{r}
2\,|\,1¢ \\
+\ 1\,|\,8¢ \\
\hline
3\,|\,9¢
\end{array}
$$

Check

Remember
43¢ + 29¢ is the same as 43 + 29.

Add.

1.
$$
\begin{array}{r}
7\,|\,2¢ \\
+\ 1\,|\,9¢ \\
\hline
9\,|\,1¢
\end{array}
$$

2.
$$
\begin{array}{r}
5\,|\,6¢ \\
+\ 2\,|\,5¢ \\
\hline
\end{array}
$$

3.
$$
\begin{array}{r}
4\,|\,3¢ \\
+\ 2\,|\,9¢ \\
\hline
\end{array}
$$

4.
$$
\begin{array}{r}
8\,|\,1¢ \\
+\ 1\,|\,7¢ \\
\hline
\end{array}
$$

5.
$$
\begin{array}{r}
5\,|\,9¢ \\
+\ 3\,|\,0¢ \\
\hline
\end{array}
$$

6.
$$
\begin{array}{r}
3\,|\,8¢ \\
+\ 4\,|\,8¢ \\
\hline
\end{array}
$$

7. **Talk About It** How is adding money different than adding two-digit numbers?

Add.

> **Remember**
> When you add money
> amounts, write the ¢
> in your answer.

8.
```
   2 5¢
 + 5 0¢
```

9.
```
   9 1¢
 +   3¢
```

10.
```
   31¢
 + 29¢
```

11.
```
   60¢
 + 11¢
```

12.
```
   85¢
 +  5¢
```

13.
```
   20¢
 + 55¢
```

14.
```
   25¢
 + 50¢
```

15.
```
   49¢
 + 29¢
```

16.
```
   45¢
 + 45¢
```

17.
```
   42¢
 + 50¢
```

18.
```
   73¢
 +  7¢
```

19.
```
   48¢
 + 16¢
```

20.
```
   95¢
 +  2¢
```

21.
```
   77¢
 + 18¢
```

Problem Solving

22. Logical Reasoning You have two quarters,
two pennies, and two nickels. Which item could
you **not** buy with these coins? Circle it.

20¢   72¢   59¢   52¢

Math at Home Activity: Find two items that are priced
at less than 50¢. Have your child add to find the total cost.

Name _____

Subtract Money

Main Idea

I will regroup to subtract money.

You subtract money the same way you subtract other numbers. Write ¢ in your answer.

Find 81¢ − 22¢.

$$\begin{array}{r} 8\,|\,1¢ \\ -\ 2\,|\,2¢ \\ \hline 5\,|\,9¢ \end{array}$$

Oh, I remember doing this! I need to regroup tens as ones.

✓ Check

Remember
40¢ − 15¢ is the same as 40 − 15.

Subtract.

1.
$$\begin{array}{r} 5\,|\,7¢ \\ -\ 2\,|\,8¢ \\ \hline 2\,|\,9¢ \end{array}$$

2.
$$\begin{array}{r} 6\,|\,6¢ \\ -\ 3\,|\,9¢ \\ \hline \end{array}$$

3.
$$\begin{array}{r} 4\,|\,0¢ \\ -\ 1\,|\,5¢ \\ \hline \end{array}$$

4.
$$\begin{array}{r} 1\,|\,3¢ \\ -\ \ \ |\,9¢ \\ \hline \end{array}$$

5.
$$\begin{array}{r} 3\,|\,9¢ \\ -\ 2\,|\,8¢ \\ \hline \end{array}$$

6.
$$\begin{array}{r} 7\,|\,8¢ \\ -\ 5\,|\,5¢ \\ \hline \end{array}$$

7. **Talk About It** How is subtracting money like subtracting other two-digit numbers?

Subtract.

8.
```
  5|0¢
- 2|6¢
```

9.
```
  6|1¢
+ 1|7¢
```

> **Remember**
> If you do not have enough ones, you will need to regroup tens as ones.

10.
```
  49¢
- 39¢
```

11.
```
  35¢
-  4¢
```

12.
```
  85¢
- 19¢
```

13.
```
  90¢
- 76¢
```

14.
```
  34¢
- 24¢
```

15.
```
  45¢
-  9¢
```

16.
```
  91¢
- 75¢
```

17.
```
  53¢
- 44¢
```

18.
```
  78¢
- 77¢
```

19.
```
  75¢
- 50¢
```

20.
```
  82¢
- 15¢
```

21.
```
  63¢
- 47¢
```

Problem Solving

22. **Number Sense** You give the lunchroom cashier 2 quarters for juice. The juice costs 42¢. How much change will you get?

_____

Math at Home Activity: Ask your child to subtract the price of two items that cost less than $1.00.

Name _____

Problem-Solving Investigation

I put 10 pennies in a row. I took out every third penny and put down a nickel. Then I picked up every fifth penny and put down a dime. How much money is in my line of coins?

Main Idea

I will choose a strategy to solve a problem.

Your Mission:
Find how much money is in Mario's line of coins.

Understand

What do I know? Underline what you know.
What do I need to find? Circle the question.

Plan

How will I solve the problem?
One way is to act it out.

Solve

Act it out.

Mario has __40¢__.

Check

Look back.
Is my answer reasonable?

▶ Mixed Problem Solving

Problem-Solving Strategies

- Act it out
- Draw a picture
- Write a number sentence

Choose a strategy. Solve.

1. Paco has 1 half dollar, 4 pennies, and 1 dime to buy a snack. How much money does he have?

   _____

2. Tess has 2 quarters. She buys a pencil for 15¢. How much money does she have now?

   _____

3. A glass of lemonade costs 50¢. Rico pays for it with 2 coins. What 2 coins does he use?

   _____

4. Riley spends 3 quarters on a drink. Then he buys a pretzel for 2 dimes. How much money does he spend?

   _____

5. Yori is saving money to buy a kite. She has 1 quarter, 1 nickel, and 2 pennies. The kite costs 75¢. How much more money does she need?

   _____

Math at Home Activity: Take advantage of problem-solving opportunities during daily routines such as riding in the car, bedtime, doing laundry, putting away groceries, planning schedules, and so on.

Today there are new designs for nickels and quarters. This table shows how many designs had been made by the end of 2006.

Coin	Number of Designs
penny	1
nickel	7
dime	1
quarter	40

If you had one nickel for every nickel design, how much money would you have?

_____ cents

FOLD DOWN

Problem Solving in Art

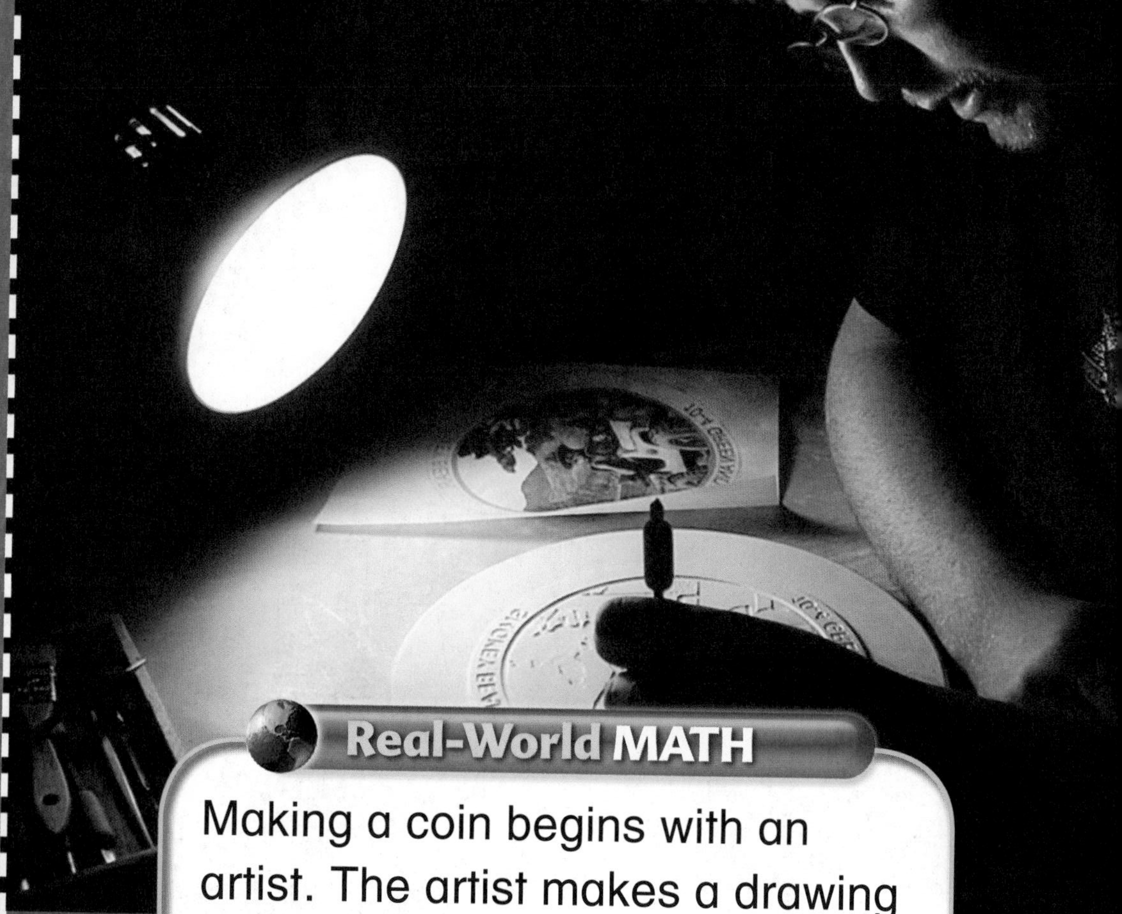

Real-World MATH

Making a coin begins with an artist. The artist makes a drawing of both sides of the coin. Then a model of the coin is made.

This book belongs to

_____

Another machine stamps new, blank coins out of sheets of metal. It is like a cookie cutter and cookies! Finally, a different machine stamps the design onto the coins.

Every detail of the model is checked. Then when everything is perfect, a machine traces the model to make it the real size of the coin.

Name _____

Vocabulary

Draw lines to match.

1. **cent**

2. **dollar sign**

3. **decimal point**

a. $1.00

b. 37¢

c. $1.00

Concepts

Count to find the value of the coins.

4.

_____¢, _____¢, _____¢, _____¢, _____¢, _____¢   _____ total

5.

_____¢, _____¢, _____¢, _____¢, _____¢   _____ total

6.

_____, _____, _____, _____, _____, _____, _____   _____ total

7.

_____, _____, _____, _____, _____, _____   _____ total

Count to find the value. Do you have enough money to buy the item? Circle *yes* or *no*.

8.

yes

no

83¢

_____, _____, _____, _____, _____

Add or subtract.

9.   54¢
   + 19¢

10.   88¢
   − 8¢

11.   27¢
   + 72¢

12.   47¢
   − 11¢

13.   99¢
   − 3¢

14.   89¢
   + 5¢

15.   75¢
   − 25¢

16.   35¢
   + 36¢

Problem Solving

17. Tanya buys a pencil for 35 cents. She gives the clerk 75 cents. How much change should she get?

Tanya should get _____.

18. Trevor wants to write sixty-two cents using the cent sign. How can he write it?

_____

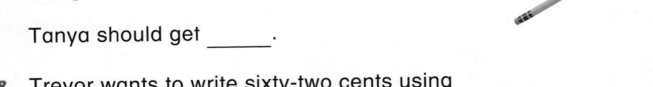

Summative Assessment

Name _____

Listen as your teacher reads each problem.
Choose the correct answer.

1. Look at the groups of coins. Which group of coins has the greatest value?

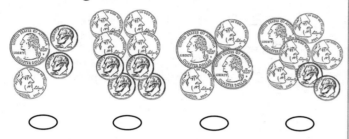

○   ○   ○   ○

2. Mirna has a quarter, a dime, and a nickel. How much money does she have?

35¢   40¢   45¢   50¢
○   ○   ○   ○

3. How many cents do these stickers cost in all?

12¢   21¢   22¢   32¢
○   ○   ○   ○

4. What is another way to write ten cents?

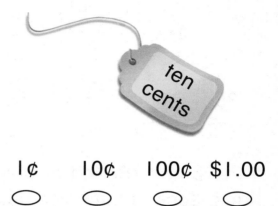

1¢   10¢   100¢ $1.00
○   ○   ○   ○

5. Percy buys a pencil for 22¢. He pays with 1 half dollar. How much change should he get back?

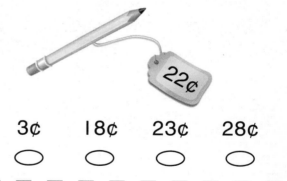

3¢   18¢   23¢   28¢
○   ○   ○   ○

6. Manny has 1 quarter, 2 dimes, 1 nickel, and 3 pennies. How much money does he have?

30¢   48¢   53¢ $1.00
○   ○   ○   ○

7. Bob has the money you see in the box. How much money is this?

25¢   30¢   40¢   50¢
○   ○   ○   ○

---

8. Lenora has 75¢ in her piggy bank. Look at the coins below. Which group could be the coins in Lenora's piggy bank?

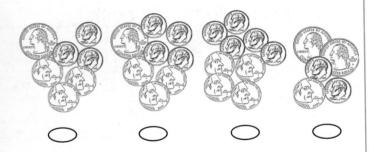

○   ○   ○   ○

---

9. What is another way to write twenty-five cents?

25¢   52¢   205¢ $2.05
○   ○   ○   ○

---

10. Which of these can be used to check the answer to the problem in the box?

$$5 + 4 = 9$$

6 + 3 = 9   13 − 4 = 9
○   ○

9 + 4 = 13   9 − 5 = 4
○   ○

---

11. Lola has the money you see in the box. How much money is this?

_____ cents

---

12. Heather had $54. She bought milk for $2. She bought a salad for lunch. Then she had $46 left. How much did the salad cost?

_____

STOP

Summative Assessment

CHAPTER 8

Measure Time and Temperature

Key Vocabulary
- temperature
- second
- minute
- hour

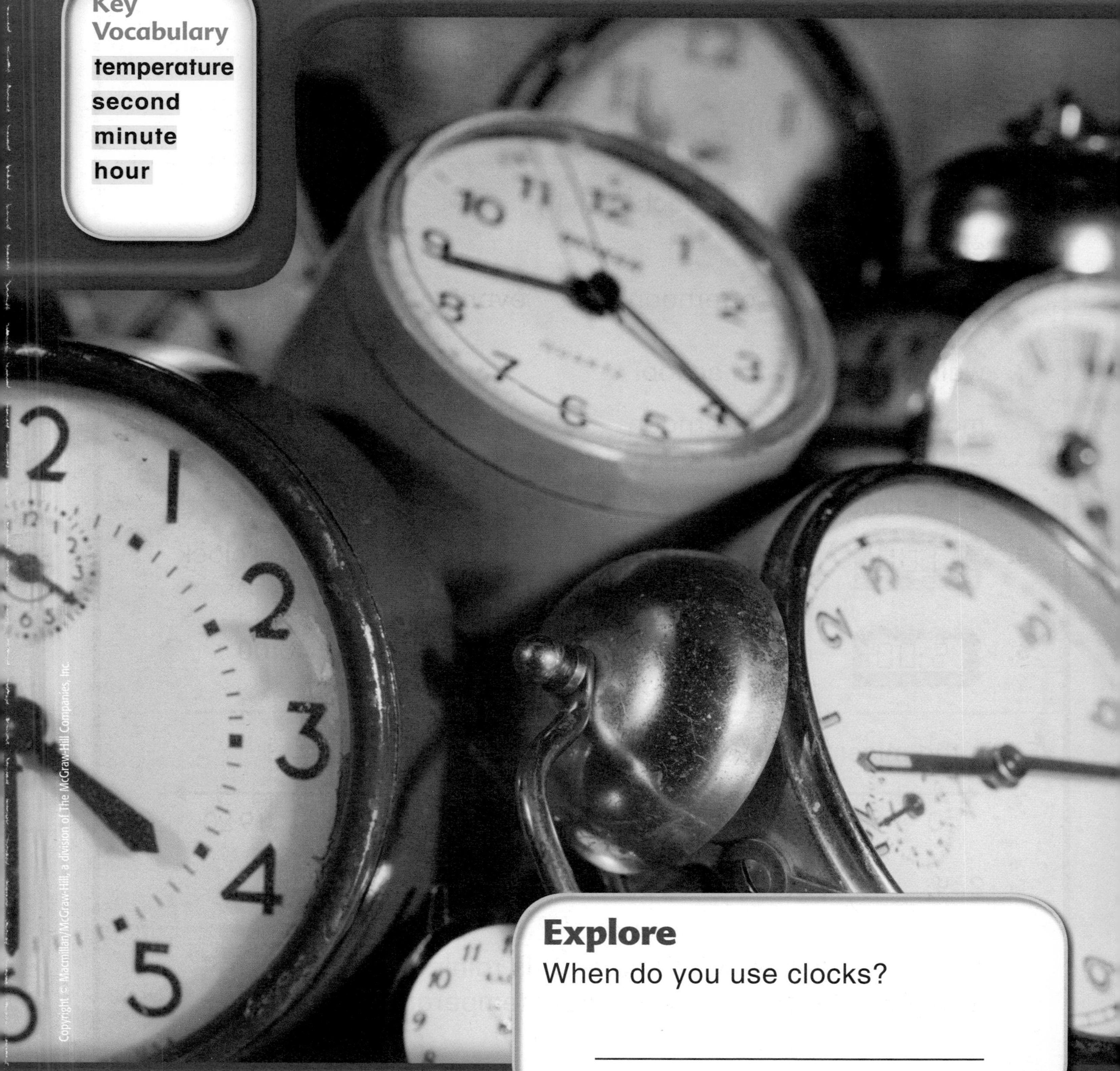

Explore

When do you use clocks?

____

Name _____

Are You Ready for Chapter 8?

Circle the activity that takes **more** time.

1. washing your hands   washing a car

2. going on vacation   going to the store

Circle the time of day for each activity.

3. eating breakfast

    morning   afternoon   evening

4. walking home from school

    morning   afternoon   evening

Circle the time.

5. `7:00`   7 o'clock   2 o'clock   6 o'clock

6. `5:00`   4:00   5:00   6:00

Fill in the missing numbers.

7.
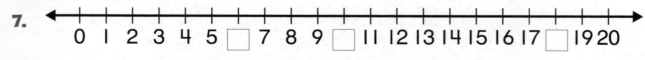

0 1 2 3 4 5 ☐ 7 8 9 ☐ 11 12 13 14 15 16 17 ☐ 19 20

2, 4, _____, 8, _____, 12, 14, 16, _____, 20

8. It is snowing in New York City. It is raining
in Dallas. Which city has a colder temperature?

_____

This page checks skills needed for Chapter 8.

Dear Family,

Today my class started Chapter 8, **Measure Time and Temperature.** In this chapter, I will learn to read and write time and temperature. Here is an activity we can do and a list of books we can read together.

Love, _____

Activity

Have your child use a thermometer to measure the temperature at 7:00 A.M., 12:00 P.M., and 5:00 P.M. Record your findings on a chart.

Time	Temp
7:00	72°F
12:00	76°F
5:00	

Key Vocabulary

temperature a measure of how hot or cold something is

minute a unit of time equal to 60 seconds

hour a unit of time equal to 60 minutes

Math Online Click on the eGlossary link at <u>macmillanmh.com</u> to find out more about these words. There are 13 languages.

Books to Read

Clocks and More Clocks
by Pat Hutchins
Aladdin, 1994.

Bats Around the Clock
by Kathy Appelt
HarperCollins,
2000.

My Grandmother's Clock
by Geraldine McCaughrean
Clarion Books,
2002.

Estimada familia:

Hoy mi clase comenzó el Capítulo 8, **Mide el tiempo y la temperatura.** En este capítulo, aprenderé a leer y a escribir la hora y la temperatura. A continuación, hay una actividad que podemos hacer y una lista de libros que podemos leer juntos.

Cariños, _____

Actividad

Pidan a su hijo(a) que use un termómetro para medir la temperatura a las 7:00 A.M. y a las 5:00 P.M. Anoten las medidas en una tabla.

Tiempo	Temperatura
7:00	72°F
12:00	76°F
5:00	

Vocabulario clave

temperatura una medida del grado de calor o frío de algún cuerpo

minuto una unidad que se usa para medir el tiempo

hora unidad de tiempo que equivale a 60 minutos

Math Online Visiten el enlace eGlossary en macmillanmh.com para averiguar más sobre estas palabras, las cuales se muestran en 13 idiomas.

Libros recomendados

Compartiendo igualmente
de Hollie J. Endress
Capstone Press, 2006.

¡Todos ganan!
de Sheila Bruce
The Kane Press, 2005.

Grupos desfilando
de Mel Campbell
Rourke Publishing, LLC., 2006.

Read Temperature

Get Ready

Main Idea

I will estimate temperature and read a thermometer.

Vocabulary

temperature
thermometer
degree
Fahrenheit

Some thermometers show every degree. Other thermometers skip count by 2s or 5s. In this chapter, we will use thermometers that show every degree.

Temperature is how hot or cold something is. You can use a **thermometer** to measure temperature. The marks on the thermometer show the **degrees Fahrenheit** (°F).

°Fahrenheit
110°
100°
90°
80°
70°
60°
50°
40°
30°
20°
10°
0°
−5°

A Hot Day

91 °F

A Cool Day

56 °F

A Cold Day

15 °F

Check

Write the temperature.

1.

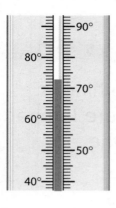

_____ °F

2.

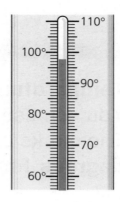

_____ °F

3.

_____ °F

4.

_____ °F

Estimate the temperature in each picture.
Circle the temperature.

5.

30°F   57°F   80°F

6.

2°F   38°F   77°F

7. **Talk About It** How do you read a thermometer? Explain.

GO on

Name _____

Write the temperature.

8.

_____

9.

_____

10.

_____

11.
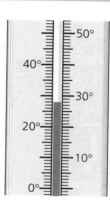
_____

Estimate the temperature in each picture.
Circle the temperature.

12.

| 15°F | 45°F | 92°F |

13.

| 8°F | 53°F | 89°F |

14. Use a thermometer to measure the temperature five days in a row. Try to measure the temperature at the same time each day. Record your data in the chart.

Day	Day 1	Day 2	Day 3	Day 4	Day 5
Time					
Temperature					

Problem Solving

15. **Critical Thinking** Read the thermometer. Draw a picture to show what you would wear outside.

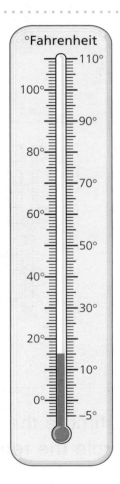

16. Write a sentence to explain your picture.

_____

_____

17. How would your picture be different if the thermometer showed 75°F? Explain.

_____

_____

Math at Home Activity: Help your child use a thermometer to measure the temperature before school and before bedtime. Subtract to find the difference in temperature.

Name _____

Estimate Time

Main Idea

I will estimate time and describe events in seconds, minutes, and hours.

Vocabulary

second

minute

hour

Time Relationships

60 **seconds** = I **minute**

60 minutes = I **hour**

I second

Sneezing takes about I second.

I minute

Washing your face takes about I minute.

I hour

Shopping for groceries takes about I hour.

Estimate the time it takes to tie your shoes.

I second    I minute   I hour

Estimate the time for each event. Circle your answer.

1. packing your book bag

I second   I minute   I hour

2. playing at the park

I second   I minute   I hour

3. reading a book

I second   I minute   I hour

4. smiling at a friend

I second   I minute   I hour

5. shaking hands

I second   I minute   I hour

6. brushing your hair

I second   I minute   I hour

7. **Talk About It** Name events that take a second, a minute, and an hour.

GO on

Name _____

Think
1 minute = 60 seconds
1 hour = 60 minutes

Estimate the time for each event. Circle your answer.

8. watching 2 television shows

1 second   1 minute   1 hour

9. crossing the monkey bars

1 second   1 minute   1 hour

10. singing a song

1 second   1 minute   1 hour

11. turning out the light

1 second   1 minute   1 hour

12. taking a test

1 second   1 minute   1 hour

13. making a sandwich

1 second   1 minute   1 hour

14. **WRITING IN ► MATH** Rita made a
to-do list for tonight. Help Rita sort her tasks
by the amount of time each task takes.

Rita's To-Do List	
I second	_____ _____
I minute	_____ _____
I hour	_____ _____

Notepad:
- wash my hands
- help make dinner
- go to dance lessons
- brush my teeth
- say goodnight
- close door

15. Make your own to-do list on the notepad.
Name tasks that take about I second, I minute,
and I hour. Sort your tasks on the chart.
Write at least two tasks under each time.

My To-Do List	
I second	_____ _____
I minute	_____ _____
I hour	_____ _____

Math at Home Activity: Help your child to prepare a daily schedule.
Have your child estimate the time it will take to complete each task on the
schedule.

Name _____

Time to the Hour and Half Hour

Get Ready

Main Idea

I will use a clock to tell time to the hour and half hour.

Vocabulary

half hour

Review Vocabulary

hour

60 minutes = 1 hour

In 1 hour, the minute hand makes a complete circle around a clock. The hour hand moves from one number to the next.

Read the time as **ten o'clock.**

Write the time.

30 minutes = a **half hour**

In a half hour, the minute hand makes it halfway around a clock. The hour hand moves halfway to the next number.

Read the time as **half past 10.**

Write the time.

✓ Check

Read the time. Write the time.

1.

2.

3. **Talk About It**   At 1:30, where is the minute hand pointing? Where is the hour hand pointing? Explain.

Read the time. Write the time.

4.

5.

6.

7.

Read the time. Then draw the minute hand. Use to help.

8. half past 1

9. 7 o'clock

10. 11 o'clock

11. half past 10

Data File

The Dauphin Island Sea Lab teaches children about plants and animals that live along the Alabama coast. The lab's aquarium contains many animals from the Gulf of Mexico.

12. The aquarium is open from 9 o'clock to 5 o'clock. Show the times on the clocks below.

Math at Home Activity: Ask your child to tell you the time at 6:00. Ask your child what time it will be in 30 minutes and 30 minutes after that.

Name _____

Problem-Solving Strategy
Look for a Pattern

Main Idea

I will look for patterns to solve a problem.

On Saturdays, there is a baseball game every 3 hours at Post Park. The first game starts at 7:00. What time will the third game start?

Understand

What do I know? Underline what you know.
What do I need to find? Circle the question.

Plan

How will I solve the problem? I will identify the pattern rule. Then I will use the rule to continue the pattern.

Solve

Look for a pattern.

The third game takes place at _____ : _____ _____.

Check

Look back.
Is my answer reasonable?

Try It

Look for a pattern to solve.

1. The second graders are performing three plays. The first play is at 10:00. The second play is at 12:00. If the plays are equally spaced, what time will the third play begin?

_____

2. The art museum offers 4 tours each day. The tours take place every 2 hours. The first tour starts at 9:30. What time does the last tour begin?

_____

Your Turn

Look for a pattern to solve.

3. Every half hour, a bus picks up people at the bus stop. The first bus arrives at 8:00. What time will the fourth bus arrive?

_____

4. Vera wants to see a movie at the theater. The first three showtimes were at 11:30, 2:30, and 5:30. If the pattern continues, what time will the next show begin?

_____

Math at Home Activity: Look at the television guide. Ask your child to identify a time pattern.

Name _____

Write the temperature.

1. 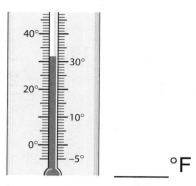 _____ °F

2. 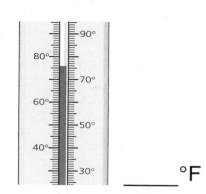 _____ °F

3.  _____ °F

Estimate the temperature in the picture. Circle your answer.

4.

20°F   45°F   85°F

Estimate the time for this event. Circle your answer.

5. picking up the phone

I second   I minute   I hour

Read the time. Draw the minute hand.

6. seven o'clock

7. half past five

8. eight o'clock

9. Isabel needs to be at the movie 30 minutes after six o'clock. What time does Isabel need to be at the movie?

_____ : _____ _____

Add or subtract.

10.
```
   29
+  11
```

11.
```
   62
+  16
```

12.
```
   48
+  23
```

13.
```
   82
-  17
```

14.
```
   37
-  21
```

15.
```
   52¢
+  42¢
```

16.
```
   73¢
+  26¢
```

17.
```
   11¢
+   6¢
```

18.
```
   64¢
-  36¢
```

19.
```
   37¢
-  14¢
```

Students collected leaves for a project. Use the tally
chart to complete the picture graph. Answer the questions.

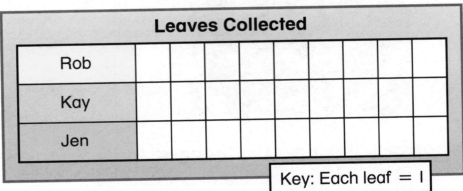

Students	Tally
Rob	卌 |||
Kay	卌	
Jen	||||

Leaves Collected

Rob								
Kay								
Jen								

Key: Each leaf = 1

20. Who collected the most leaves? _____

21. How many leaves did Kay and Jen collect? _____ leaves

22. How many more leaves did Rob collect than Jen? _____ leaves

23. Matt wants to know how many dishes he has
washed. One day he washed 12. The next day
he washed 20. The last day he washed 17.
How many dishes did Matt wash?

_____ dishes

Formative Assessment

Time to the Quarter Hour

Hands-On Activity

Get Ready

Main Idea

I will use a clock to tell time to the quarter hour.

Vocabulary

quarter hour

There are 15 minutes in a **quarter hour**.
Use a clock to measure time to the quarter hour.

1 o'clock	quarter past 1	half past 1	quarter till 2

1:00   1:15   1:30   1:45

Check

Use your . Read the time. Then draw the minute hand.

1.

11:15

2.

8:30

3.

10:45

4.

6:45

5.

4:15

6.

9:30

7. **Talk About It** At 4:15, where is the minute hand? Explain.

Practice

Use your . Read the time. Then draw the minute hand.

8.
7:45

9.
12:30

10.
2:15

11.
1:45

12.
3:30

13.
6:00

14.
12:45

15.
5:00

16.
4:15

H.O.T. Problem

17. **Thinking Math** Why is each 15-minute period called a quarter?

_____

_____

Math at Home Activity: Look at an analog clock. Ask your child to tell you the time at 6:15, 7:30, and 8:45.

Name _____

Time to Five-Minute Intervals

Get Ready

Main Idea

I will skip count by fives to tell time.

You can skip count by 5s to tell the time.

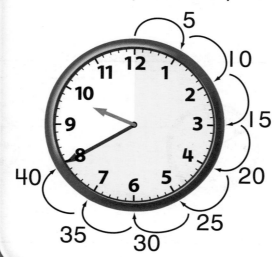

This clock shows __40__ minutes after 9 o'clock.

Write the time another way.

Check

Read the time. Then write the time. Use to help.

1.

_____ : _____ _____

2.

_____ : _____ _____

3.

_____ : _____ _____

Make each time on . Draw the minute hand to show the time.

4.

5.

6.

7. **Talk About It** Explain how you skip count by 5s to tell time.

Read the time. Then write the time. Use to help.

8.

_____ : _____ _____

9.

_____ : _____ _____

10.

_____ : _____ _____

11.

_____ : _____ _____

12.

_____ : _____ _____

13.

_____ : _____ _____

Make each time on . Draw the minute hand to show the time.

14.

15.

16.

Problem Solving

17. **Number Sense** Time is not written as 11:60. Explain why.

_____

_____

Math at Home Activity: Look at a clock with your child on the hour. Ask your child what time it will be in 5 minutes, 10 minutes, 25 minutes, and 50 minutes.

Name _____

Each animal's alarm clock is set for a different time.
Draw a line to connect each sleeping animal to the
clock that shows the time they need to get up.

1.  6:55

A.

2.  9:15

B.

3.  7:30

C.

4.  8:40

D.

5.  7:20

E.

Time to Feast

Time

Play with a partner. Take turns.
- ○ Start at half past 4.
- ○ Find the time that comes next, and write it on the oven's clock.
- ○ Make that time on your clock.
- ○ If you are correct, color the oven.
- ○ Play until all ovens are colored.

What You Need

- ○ 2
- ○  crayon
- ○  crayon

half past 4

quarter past 5

five minutes past 5

quarter till 6

ten minutes after 6

quarter till 5

5 o'clock

quarter till 7

Use a Thermometer to Gather Data

Get Ready

Main Idea

I will use a thermometer to gather data.

Students at Pine Ridge Elementary measured the temperature each morning for four days.

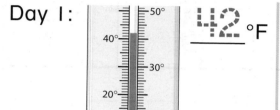

Day 1: 42 °F   Day 2: 43 °F

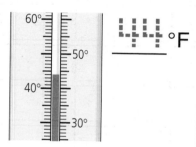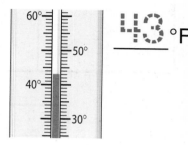

Day 3: 44 °F   Day 4: 45 °F

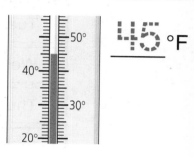

A bar graph can help you organize and compare data.

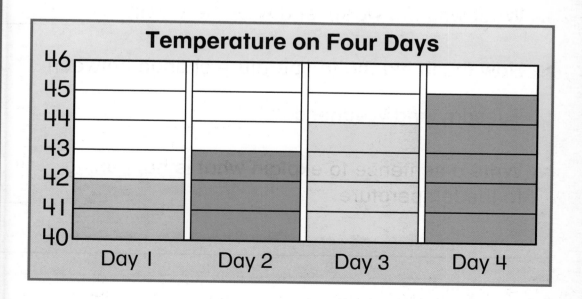

Temperature on Four Days

Students at Gray Elementary School measured the
temperature for 1 week. Use their data to fill in the bar graph.

Monday	Tuesday	Wednesday	Thursday	Friday
70° 60° 50° 40°	70° 60° 50° 40°	70° 60° 50° 40°	70° 60° 50° 40°	60° 50° 40° 30°

Weekly Temperatures

Monday										
Tuesday										
Wednesday										
Thursday										
Friday										

50 51 52 53 54 55 56 57 58 59 60

1. What was the warmest day of the week? _____

2. How much did the temperature change between

   Tuesday and Wednesday? _____

3. Write a sentence to explain what is happening
   to the temperature.

   _____

4. **Talk About It** Why might someone want to collect
   temperature data?

GO on

Name _____

Hans made a chart to show the average temperatures for every week in July. Use his data to fill in the bar graph.

Week	Week 1	Week 2	Week 3	Week 4
Temperature	76°F	83°F	85°F	88°F

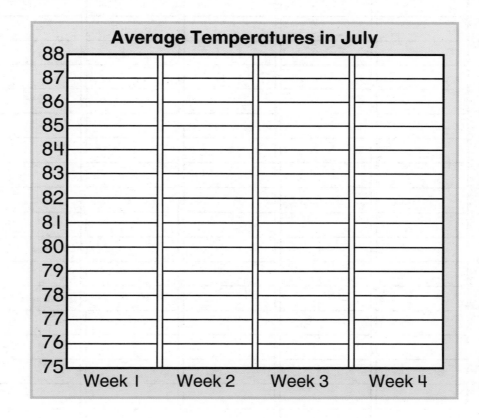

5. Which week is the hottest week in July? _____

6. How much does the average temperature change

   between Week 1 and Week 4? _____

7. Look at the bar graph. Tell about the temperatures in July.

_____

Use a thermometer to measure the temperature every
hour for 5 hours. Record your data in the chart.
Then use your data to fill in the bar graph.

Time					
Temperature					

Temperatures

100
95
90
85
80
75
70
65
60
55
50
45
40
35
30
25
20
15
10
5
0

8. What time would have been the best temperature
for a recess? Explain your answer.

_____

GO on

Name _____

> **Practice** with Technology

Use the 📊 (Level 2) to graph temperatures.

- Copy this bar graph on your computer using Math Tool Chest.

- Click and drag each bar to the correct temperature to complete the graph.

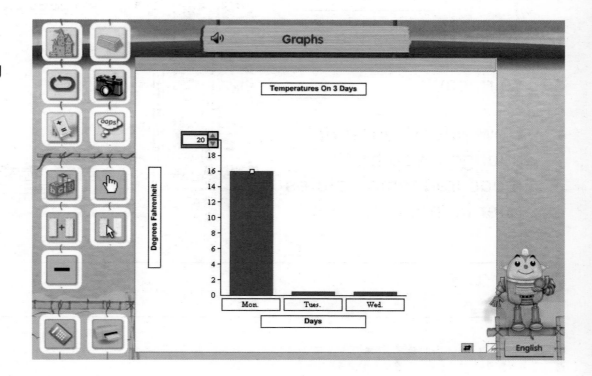

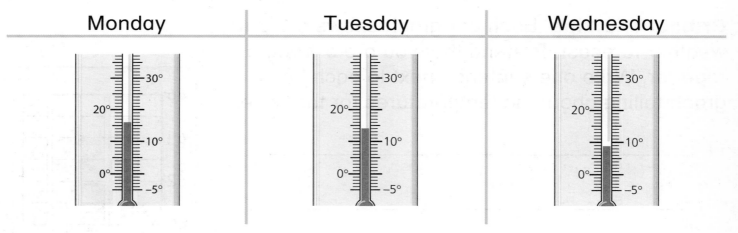

| Monday | Tuesday | Wednesday |

9. Which day was the coldest? _____

10. How would the graph change if you used temperature data from this week?

_____

_____

Use your weekly temperature data from Lesson I to make a bar graph using 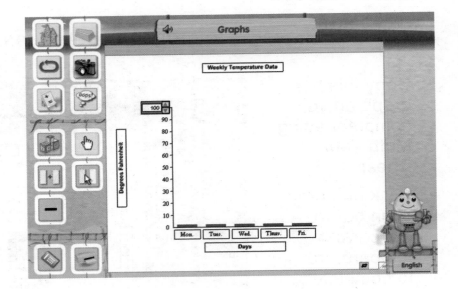.

11. Which day was the coldest? _____

12. Which day was the warmest? _____

13. How would your graph change if you had measured temperatures later in the day?

_____

_____

Problem Solving

Critical Thinking Each bar graph shows a 5-day weather forecast. Pretend that you are a weather reporter. Write one sentence next to each bar graph telling about the temperatures for that week.

14. _____

_____

_____

15. _____

_____

_____

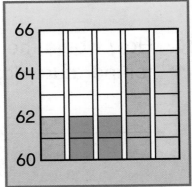

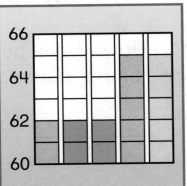

Math at Home Activity: Help your child record the temperature for 3 days. Ask your child to draw a bar graph to show the data.

Problem-Solving Investigation

Main Idea

I will make a table to solve a problem.

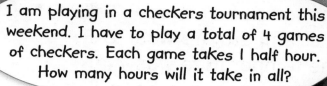

I am playing in a checkers tournament this weekend. I have to play a total of 4 games of checkers. Each game takes 1 half hour. How many hours will it take in all?

Your Mission:
Find out how many hours the tournament will take in all.

Understand

What do I know? Underline what you know.
What do I need to find? Circle the question.

Plan

How will I solve the problem?
One way is to make a table.

Solve

Make a table.

The tournament will take _____.

Check

Look back.
Is my answer reasonable?

Mixed Problem Solving

Problem-Solving
Strategies

• Make a table
• Act it out
• Draw a picture

Choose a strategy. Solve.

1. At 1:00, the temperature was 75°F.
   At 3:00, the temperature was 73°F.
   At 5:00, the temperature was 71°F.
   If this pattern continues, what will
   the temperature be at 7:00?

   _____ °F

2. Kevin has 3 classes in a row. Each class is
   2 hours long. Kevin's first class is at 7:00.
   When will Kevin's last class end?

   _____

3. It was 32°F at 7:00. The temperature increased
   3° every hour until 12:00. What was the temperature
   at 12:00?

   _____ °F

4. It takes Tasha 15 minutes to read 7 pages.
   How many pages will Tasha be able to read
   in 1 hour?

   _____ pages

Math at Home Activity: Take advantage of problem-solving
opportunities during daily routines such as riding in the car, bedtime,
doing laundry, putting away groceries, planning schedules, and so on.

D

Mr. Robinson hit 137 homeruns! In 1997 his number was retired by all major league teams.

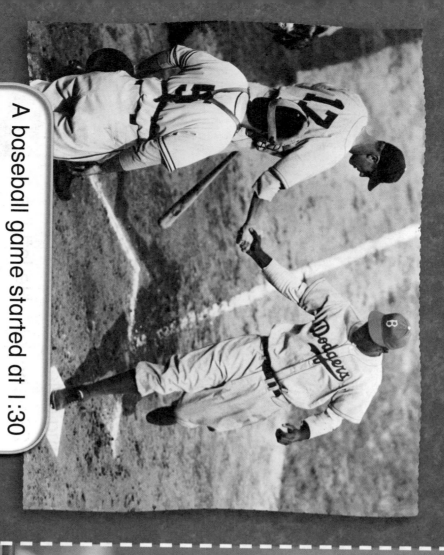

A baseball game started at 1:30 and lasted 3 hours. What time did the game end?

___ : ___

FOLD DOWN

A

Problem Solving
in Social Studies

Real-World MATH

Baseball is known as America's favorite pastime. Have you ever played baseball?

This book belongs to

_____

He started playing baseball in the major leagues when he was 28 years old. He left the major leagues when he was 37 years old. How long did he play in the major leagues?

—— years

Jackie Robinson was a famous baseball player.

Name _____

Vocabulary

Match. Write the letter by the word.

1. **hour** _____   **a.** equal to 60 minutes

2. **quarter hour** _____   **b.** used to measure temperature

3. **thermometer** _____   **c.** equal to 15 minutes

Concepts

Estimate the time for each event. Circle your answer.

4. playing a basketball game

1 second   1 minute   1 hour

5. blinking your eyes

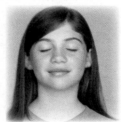

1 second   1 minute   1 hour

Write the time.

6.

7.

8.

Draw the minute hand to show the time.

9.

10.

11.

Write the time.

12.

____ : ____ ____

13.

____ : ____ ____

14.

____ : ____ ____

Problem Solving

Write the temperature. Then use the data to complete the bar graph.

15. Spring
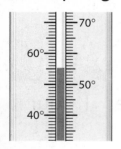

____

16. Summer
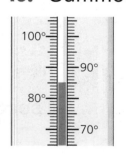

____

17. Fall

____

Temperatures									
Spring									
Summer									
Fall									

50 55 60 65 70 75 80 85 90

18. What is the difference between the summer temperature and the fall temperature?

_____

Summative Assessment

Name _____

Listen as your teacher reads each problem.
Choose the correct answer.

1. Haley's school day ends at the time shown on the clock. Find the time that is shown on the clock.

2:30   2:25   2:20   2:15
○   ○   ○   ○

2. Larry's basketball practice starts at half past 5. Look at the clocks below. Which clock shows half past 5?

○   **3:50**

○   **5:03**

○   **5:15**

○   **5:30**

3. Look at the thermometers. Find the thermometer that shows a temperature of 60 degrees.

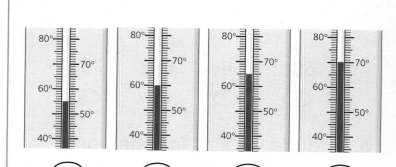

○   ○   ○   ○

4. About how long does it take to play a soccer game?

○   I second

○   25 seconds

○   I minute

○   I hour

5. Look at the coins. Find the value of the coins.

63¢   64¢   66¢   70¢

◯   ◯   ◯   ◯

6. Maude walked for one hour. How many minutes did Maude walk?

12   24   60   72

◯   ◯   ◯   ◯

7. About how long does it take to brush your teeth?

I second   I minute

◯   ◯

45 minutes   I hour

◯   ◯

8. Kylie's favorite television show starts at the time shown on the clock. Find the time that is shown on the clock.

8:06   8:30   9:00   9:30

◯   ◯   ◯   ◯

9. What is the value of the four in forty-six?

_____

10. Look at the thermometer below. What is the temperature on the thermometer?

_____ degrees

STOP

Summative Assessment

Glossary/Glosario

English	A	**Español**

add (addition) Join together sets to find the total or sum. The opposite of *subtract.* (page 55)

$$2 + 5 = 7$$

suma (adición) Unir conjuntos para calcular el total o la suma. Lo opuesto a la *resta.*

$$2 + 5 = 7$$

---

addend Any numbers or quantities being added together. (page 55)

In $2 + 3 = 5$, 2 is an addend and 3 is an addend.

$$2 + 3 = 5$$
↑   ↑

sumando Cualquier número o cantidad que se suma.

En $2 + 3 = 5$, 2 es un sumando y 3 es un sumando.

$$2 + 3 = 5$$
↑   ↑

---

after Follow in place or time. (page 33)

5 **6** 7 8

6 is just *after* 5

después Que sigue en lugar o en tiempo.

5 **6** 7 8

6 viene inmediatamente después

---

area The space inside a shape or figure. (page 395)

The area of this rectangle is 6 square units.

área Espacio dentro de una forma o figura.

El area de este rectángulo es de 6 unidades cuadradas.

---

array Objects displayed in rows and columns. (page 481)

row →

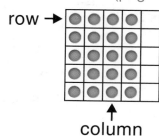

column

arreglo Objetos presentados en filas y columnas.

fila →

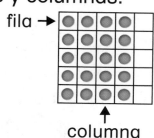

columna

Glossary/Glosario

English		Español

bar graph A graph that uses bars to show data. (page 127)

gráfica de barras Gráfica que usa barras para mostrar datos.

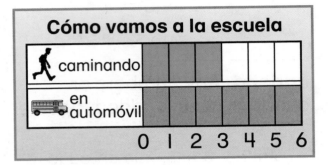

How We Get To School

Walk
Ride
0 1 2 3 4 5 6

Cómo vamos a la escuela

caminando
en automóvil
0 1 2 3 4 5 6

---

before (page 33)

5 6 7 8

6 is just *before* 7

antes

5 6 7 8

6 viene inmediate mente antes del 7

---

between (page 33)

47 48 49 50

49 is *between* 48 and 50

entre

47 48 49 50

49 está entre 47 y 50

---

capacity The amount of dry or liquid material a container can hold. (page 409)

capacidad Cantidad de material seco o líquido que puede contener un recipiente.

---

cent (¢) (page 211)

1¢   1 cent

centavo (¢)

1¢   1 centavo

Glossary/Glosario

English		Español

centimeter (cm) A metric unit for measuring length. (page 391)

centimeters

centímetro (cm) Una unidad métrica de medida alturas.

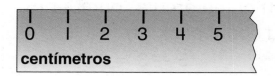
centímetros

circle A closed, round plane shape. (page 351)

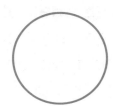

círculo Figura redonda y cerrada.

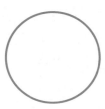

compare Look at objects, shapes, or numbers and see how they are alike or different.

(page 35)

comparar Observar objetos, formas o números y ver en qué se parecen o en qué se diferencian.

cone A solid shape that narrows to a point from a circular base.

(page 345)

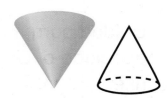

cono Figura sólida que se estrecha hasta formar un punto desde una base circular.

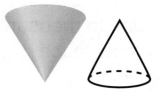

coordinate graph A graph with points to show data.

(page 367)

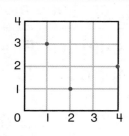

gráfica de coordenadas Gráfica con puntos para mostrar datos.

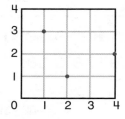

Glossary/Glosario

English   ## Español

C

count back On a number line, start at the greater number (5) and count back (3). (page 87)

$$5 - 3 = 2$$

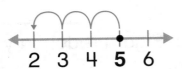

2 3 4 **5** 6

contar al revés En una recta numérica, comienza en el número 5 y cuenta 3 al revés.

$$5 - 3 = 2$$

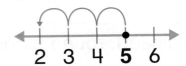

2 3 4 **5** 6

---

count on (or count up) Start at a number on a number line and count up to the next number. (page 57)

$$4 + 2 = 6$$

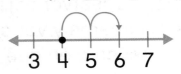

3 4 5 6 7

contar hacia adelante Comenzar en una recta numéricarecta numérica y contar hacia adelante hasta el siguiente número.

$$4 + 2 = 6$$

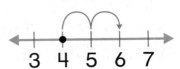

3 4 5 6 7

---

cube A solid shape with 6 square faces. (page 345)

cubo Figura tridimensional con 6 caras cuadradas.

---

cup (c) A unit to measure capacity or how much something holds. (page 411)

 A small paper cup holds about 1 cup.

taza (tz) Unidad para medir la capacidad o cuánto contiene algo.

 Una taza de cartón pequeña contiene más o menos 1 taza.

---

cylinder A solid shape that looks like a can. (page 345)

cilindro Figura sólida con forma de lata.

Glossary/Glosario

English		Español

data Numbers or symbols, sometimes collected from a survey or experiment, that show information. *Data* is plural.

(page 117)

datos Números o símbolos que, a veces, se recopilan mediante una encuesta o experimento, para mostrar información. *Datos* es un nombre plural.

Name	Number of Pets
Mary	3
James	1
Alonzo	4

Nombre	Número de mascotas
Maria	3
James	1
Alonzo	4

---

decimal point A period used in a decimal number. (page 223)

$2.95
↑

punto decimal Punto que se utiliza en un número decimal.

$2.95
↑

---

degree (°) A unit of measure for temperature. (page 245)

grado (°) Unidad para medir la temperatura.

---

difference The answer to a subtraction problem. (page 87)

$$3 - 1 = 2$$
↑

The difference is 2.

diferencia Resultado de un problema de sustracción.

$$3 - 1 = 2$$
↑

La diferencia es 2.

---

digit A symbol used to write numbers. The ten digits are 0, 1, 2, 3, 4, 5, 6, 7, 8, 9. (page 21)

dígito Símbolo que se utiliza para representar números. Los diez dígitos son 0, 1, 2, 3, 4, 5, 6, 7, 8, 9.

Glossary/Glosario

English		Español

English

dime dime = 10¢ or 10 cents (page 211)

head   tail

divide (division) To separate into equal groups. (page 487)

9 ÷ 3 = 3

division sentence A math sentence that has a division sign in it. (page 489)

12 ÷ 3 = 4

dollar one dollar =100¢ or 100 cents. Also written as $1.00. (page 223)

front

back

dollar sign ($) A symbol used to show dollar amounts. (page 223)

 three dollars = $3

Español

moneda de 10 centavos moneda de 10 centavos = 10¢ ó 10 centavos

cara   escudo

dividir (división) Separar en grupos iguales.

9 ÷ 3 = 3

enunciado de división Enunciado matemático que contiene un signo de división.

12 ÷ 3 = 4

dólar un dólar = 100¢ ó 100 centavos

frente

dorso

signo de dólar ($) Símbolo que se utiliza para mostrar las cantidades de dólares.

$ tres dólares = $3

Glossary/Glosario

English	D	**Español**

doubles (and near doubles)
Two addends that are the same number. (page 63)

$6 + 6 = 12$ ← doubles
$6 + 7 = 13$ ← near doubles

dobles (y casi dobles) Dos sumandos que son el mismo número.

$7 + 7 = 14$ ← dobles
$7 + 8 = 15$ ← casi dobles

E

edge The line where two *sides* or *faces* meet. (page 347)

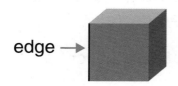

edge →

arista La línea donde se encuentran dos lados *o caras*.

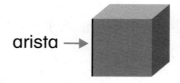

arista →

equal groups Each group has the same number of objects. (page 475)

There are four equal groups of counters.

grupos iguales Cada grupo tiene el mismo número de objetos.

Hay cuatro grupos iguales de fichas.

equal parts Each part is the same size. (page 283)

This sandwich is cut into 2 equal parts.

partes iguales Cada parte es del mismo tamaño.

Este sándwich está cortado en 2 partes iguales.

Glossary/Glosario

English **E**	Español

estimate Find a number close to an exact amount. (page 29)

47 + 22 rounds to 50 + 20
The estimate is 70.

estimar Hallar un número cercano a la cantidad exacta.

47 + 22 se redondea a 50 + 20.
La estimación es 70.

---

expanded form
The representation of a number as a sum that shows the value of each digit. Sometimes called *expanded notation*. (page 319)

536 is written as 500 + 30 + 6.

forma desarrollada La representación de un número como suma que muestra el valor de cada dígito. Algunas veces se llama *notación desarrollada*.

536 se escribe como
500 + 30 + 6.

F

face The flat part of a 3-dimensional figure. (page 347)

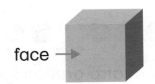

A square is a face of a cube.

cara La parte plana de una figura tridimensional.

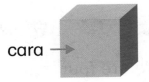

Un cuadrado es la cara de un cubo.

---

fact family Addition and subtraction sentences that use the same numbers. (page 103)

6 + 7 = 13	13 − 7 = 6
7 + 6 = 13	13 − 6 = 7

familia de operaciones Enunciados de adición y sustracción que utilizan los mismos números.

6 + 7 = 13	13 − 7 = 6
7 + 6 = 13	13 − 6 = 7

Glossary/Glosario

English		Español

Fahrenheit A customary system for measuring temperature. (page 245)

Fahrenheit Unidad del sistema inglés para medir temperaturas.

fraction A number that represents part of a whole or part of a set. (page 283)

$$\left(\frac{1}{2}\right), \left(\frac{1}{3}\right), \left(\frac{1}{4}\right), \left(\frac{3}{4}\right)$$

Fractions

fracción Número que representa la parte de un todo o la parte de un conjunto.

$$\left(\frac{1}{2}\right), \left(\frac{1}{3}\right), \left(\frac{1}{4}\right), \left(\frac{3}{4}\right)$$

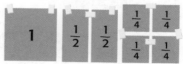

Fracciones

gallon (gal) A liquid measure of capacity. (page 411)

A milk jug contains 1 gallon.

galón (gal) Medida de capacidad liquida.

Un recipiente de leche contiene 1 galón.

gram (g) A metric unit for measuring mass. (page 425)

A paperclip weighs about 1 gram.

gramo (g) Unidad métrica para medir la masa.

Un clip pesa más o menos 1 gramo.

Glossary/Glosario

English		Español
	G	

group A set of objects (page 297)

group of 4

grupo Conjunto o grupo de elementos

grupo de 4

	H	

half-dollar half-dollar = 50¢ or 50 cents (page 215)

head   tail

medio dólar medio dólar = 50¢ ó 50 centavos

cara   escudo

half hour One half of an hour is 30 minutes. Sometimes called half past or half past the hour. (page 253)

medio hora Media hora equivale a 30 minutos. A veces, se llama y media o media hora después de la hora.

hexagon A two-dimensional figure that has six sides. (page 351)

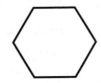

hexágono Figura que tiene seis lados.

Glossary/Glosario

English	H	Español

hour A unit of time. (page 249)

1 hour = 60 minutes

hora Unidad de tiempo.

1 hora = 60 minutos

hundreds The numbers 100–999. (page 313)

In the number 234, the 2 is in the hundreds place.

centenas Los números del 100–999.

En el número 234, el 2 está en el lugar de las centenas.

I

inch (in.) A customary unit for measuring length. The plural is *inches.* (page 381)

12 inches = 1 foot

pulgada (pulg) Unidad inglesa para medir longitud. El plural es *pulgadas.*

12 pulgadas = 1 pie

inverse Operations that undo each other. (page 97)

Addition and subtraction are inverse or opposite operations.

operación inversa Operaciones que se anulan entre sí.

La adición y la sustracción son operaciones inversas u opuestas.

is equal to = (page 35)

6 = 6

6 is equal to or the same as 6.

es igual a =

6 = 6

6 es igual a o lo mismo que 6.

Glossary/Glosario

English		**Español**

**is greater than > ** (page 35)

7 > 2

7 is greater than 2.

es mayor que >

7 > 2

7 es mayor que 2.

---

is less than < (page 35)

4 < 7

4 is less than 7.

es menor que <

4 < 7

4 es menor que 7.

K

key Tells what (or how many) each symbol stands for. (page 119)

Favorite Pet			
Fish	☺	☺	☺
Dog	☺		
Cat	☺	☺	

Key: ☺ = 2 votes

clave Indica qué o cuánto representa cada símbolo.

Animal doméstico favorito			
Pez	☺	☺	☺
Perro	☺		
Gato	☺	☺	

Clave: ☺ = 2 votes

---

kilogram (kg) A metric unit for measuring mass. (page 425)

A pair of men's shoes weighs about 1 kilogram.

kilogramo (kg) Unidad métrica para medir masa.

Un par de zapatos de caballero pesan más o menos 1 kilogramo.

Glossary/Glosario

<table>
<tr><th>English</th><th>Español</th></tr>
</table>

L

length How long or how far away something is. (page 379)

length

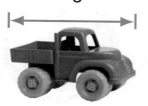

longitud La longitud de algo o a qué distancia está.

longitud

---

less likely An event that will probably not happen. (page 133)

Picking the green cube is less likely than picking a red one.

menos probable Evento que probablemente no ocurrirá.

Elegir el cubo verde es menos posible que elegir uno rojo.

---

liter (l) A metric unit of measure for volume or capacity. (page 417)

A water bottle holds about 1 liter.

litro (l) Unidad métrica para medir el volumen o la capacidad.

Una botella de agua contiene más o menos 1 litro.

M

measure To find the length, height, or weight using standard or nonstandard units. (page 379)

medir Hallar la longitud, altura o el peso usando unidades estándar o no estándar.

---

milliliter (ml) A metric unit used for measuring capacity. (page 417)

A medicine dropper holds about 1 milliliter.

mililitro (ml) Unidad métrica que se usa para medir la capacidad.

Un gotero para medicina contiene más o menos 1 mililitro.

Glossary/Glosario

English		Español

minute (min) A unit used to measure time. (page 249)

I minute = 60 seconds

minuto (min) Unidad que se usa para medir el tiempo.

I minuto = 60 segundos

---

missing addend (page 101)

$$9 + \boxed{} = 16$$

The missing addend is 7.

sumando desconocido

$$9 + \boxed{} = 16$$

El sumando desconocido es 7.

---

more likely An event will probably happen. (page 133)

You are more likely to choose a red cube.

más posible Evento que probablemente ocurrirá.

Es más posible que elijas un cubo rojo.

---

multiplication sentence A math sentence that has a multiplication sign in it. (page 479)

$$5 \times 4 = 20$$

enunciado de multiplicación Un enunciado matemático que contiene un signo de multiplicación.

$$5 \times 4 = 20$$

---

multiply (multiplication) Find the product. The operation of repeated addition of the same number. (page 473)

$$4 \times 2 = 8$$
Four groups of two are equal to eight or
$$2 + 2 + 2 + 2 = 8.$$

multiplicar (multiplicación) Calcular el producto. La operación de adición repetida del mismo número.

$$4 \times 2 = 8.$$
Cuatro grupos de dos son iguales a ocho ó
$$2 + 2 + 2 + 2 = 8.$$

Glossary/Glosario

English		**Español**

---

nickel nickel = 5¢ or 5 cents
(page 211)

head   tail

moneda de cinco centavos moneda de cinco centavos = 5¢ ó 5 centavos

cara   escudo

---

nonstandard units Objects such as blocks, paper clips, crayons, and pencils that can be used to measure. (page 379)

unidades no estándares Objetos como bloques, clips, crayones y lápices que se pueden usar para medir.

---

number line A line with number labels. (page 33)

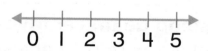

0 1 2 3 4 5

recta numéricarecta numérica Recta con rótulos de números.

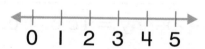

0 1 2 3 4 5

---

ones A place value of a number. (page 17)

23
This number has 3 ones.

unidades El valor de posición de un número.

23
Este número tiene 3 unidades.

---

ounce (oz) A customary unit for measuring weight or capacity.
(page 423)

One CD weighs about 1 ounce.

onza (oz) Unidad del sistema inglés para medir el peso o la capacidad.

Un CD pesa más o menos 1 onza.

Glossary/Glosario

| **English** | **P** | **Español** |

parallelogram A two-dimensional figure that has four sides. Each pair of opposite sides is equal and parallel. (page 351)

paralelogramo Figura que tiene cuatro lados. Cada par de lados opuestos es igual y paralelo.

pattern An order that a set of objects or numbers follows over and over. (page 39)

patrón Orden que sigue una y otra vez un conjunto de objetos o números.

A, A, B, A, A, B, A, A, B

A, A, B, A, A, B, A, A, B

penny penny = 1¢ or 1 cent (page 211)

moneda de un centavo Centavo = 1¢ ó 1 centavo

head   tail

cara   escudo

picture graph A graph that has different pictures to show information collected. (page 119)

gráfica de imagen Gráfica que tiene diferentes imágenes para mostrar la información recopilada.

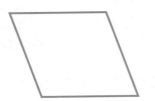

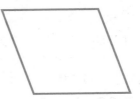

Glossary/Glosario

English		Español

P

place value The value given to a *digit* by its place in a number. (page 21)

365
3 is in the hundreds place.
6 is in the tens place.
5 is in the ones place.

valor de posición El valor dado a un *dígito* según su posición en un número.

365
3 está en el lugar de las centenas.
6 está en el lugar de las decenas.
5 está en el lugar de las unidades.

---

pound (lb) A customary unit for measuring weight or mass.

(page 423)

A box of crayons weighs about 1 pound.

libra (lb) Unidad del sistema inglés para medir el peso o la masa.

Una caja de crayones pesa más o menos 1 libra.

---

product The answer to a multiplication problem. (page 479)

$$3 \times 4 = 12$$
↑

producto Resultado de un problema de multiplicación.

$$3 \times 4 = 12$$
↑

---

pyramid A solid shape with a polygon as a base and triangular shaped faces. (page 345)

pirámide Figura sólida con un polígono como base y caras de forma triangular.

Glossary/Glosario

	English		Español

Q

quarter quarter = 25¢ or 25 cents (page 215)

head   tail

moneda de 25 centavos moneda de 25 centavos = 25¢ ó 25 centavos

cara   escudo

---

quarter hour One-fourth of an hour or 15 minutes. (page 259)

cuarto de hora Un cuarto de una hora ó 15 minutos.

R

rectangle A plane shape with four sides and four corners.

(page 351)

rectángulo Forma con cuatro lados y cuatro esquinas.

---

rectangular prism
A solid shape with faces that are rectangles. (page 345)

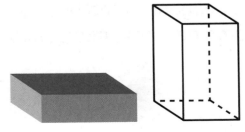

prisma rectangular Figura tridimensional con caras que son rectángulos.

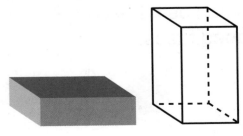

Glossary/Glosario

English	Español

regroup Take apart a number to write it in a new way. (page 153)

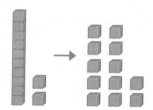

I ten + 2 ones becomes
12 ones.

reagrupar Separar un número para escribirlo de una nueva forma.

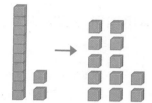

I decena + 2 unidades se convierten en 12 unidades.

---

related fact(s) Basic facts using the same numbers. Sometimes called a *fact family*.
(page 97)

$4 + 1 = 5$ $\quad$ $5 - 4 = 1$
$1 + 4 = 5$ $\quad$ $5 - 1 = 4$

operaciones relacionadas Operaciones básicas que usan los mismos números. Algunas veces se llaman *familia de operaciones*.

$4 + 1 = 5$ $\quad$ $5 - 4 = 1$
$1 + 4 = 5$ $\quad$ $5 - 1 = 4$

---

round Change the *value* of a number to one that is easier to work with. (page 163)

24 rounded to the nearest ten is 20.

redondear Cambiar el *valor* de un número a uno con el que es más fácil trabajar.

24 redondeado a la decena más cercana es 20.

S

second A unit used to measure time. (page 249)

I second = the time it takes to sneeze

segundo Unidad que se utiliza para medir el tiempo.

I segundo = el tiempo que toma estornudar

Glossary/Glosario

English	S	Español

side One of the line segments that make up a shape. (page 357)

A pentagon has five sides.

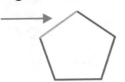

lado Uno de los segmentos de recta que componen una forma.

Un pentágono tiene cinco lados.

---

skip count Count objects in equal groups of two or more. (page 43)

2, 4, 6, 8, 10

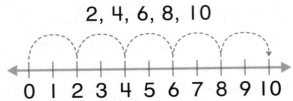

contar salteado Contar objetos en grupos iguales de dos o más.

2, 4, 6, 8, 10

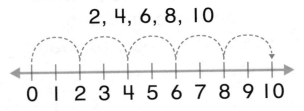

---

sphere A solid shape that has the shape of a round ball.

(page 345)

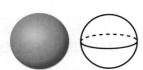

esfera Figura sólida que tiene la forma de pelota redonda.

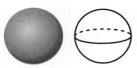

---

square A *rectangle* that has four equal sides. (page 351)

cuadrado *Rectángulo* que tiene cuatro lados iguales.

Glossary/Glosario

English		Español

subtract (subtraction) Take away, take apart, separate, or find the difference between two sets. The opposite of *addition*.

(page 87)

$$5 - 5 = 0$$

restar (sustracción) Eliminar, quitar, separar o calcular la diferencia entre dos conjuntos. Lo opuesto de la *adición*.

$$5 - 5 = 0$$

---

sum The answer to an addition problem. (page 55)

$$2 + 4 = 6$$

suma Resultado de un problema de adición.

$$2 + 4 = 6$$

---

survey Collect data by asking people the same question.

(page 117)

Favorite Animal	
Dog	卌 I
Cat	卌

This survey shows favorite animals.

encuesta Recopilar datos al hacer las mismas preguntas a las personas.

Animal Favorito	
Perro	卌 I
Gato	卌

Esta encuesta muestra los animal favoritos.

---

symbol A letter or figure that stands for something. (page 119)

This symbol means to add.

+

símbolo Letra o figura que representa algo.

Este símbolo significa sumar.

+

Glossary/Glosario

English		Español

tally mark(s) A mark used to record data collected in a survey.

(page 117)

tally marks

marca(s) de conteo Marca que se utiliza para registrar los datos recopilados en una encuesta.

marcas de conteo

---

temperature A measure of how hot or cold something is.

(page 245)

The temperature is 79 degrees.

temperatura Medida del grado de calor o frío de algo.

La temperatura es de 79 grados.

---

tens A place value of a number. (page 17)

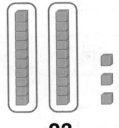

23

The 2 is in the tens place.

decenas El valor de posición de un número.

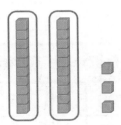

23

El 2 está en el lugar de las decenas.

---

thermometer A tool that measures how hot or cold something is (the temperature).

(page 245)

termómetro Herramienta que mide el grado de calor o frío de algo (la temperatura).

Glossary/Glosario

thousand A place value of a number. (page 323)

1,253
The 1 is in the thousands place.

millar El valor de posición de un número.

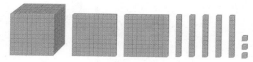

1,253
El 1 está en el lugar de los millares.

---

three-dimensional figure A shape having the three dimensions: length, width, and height. (page 345)

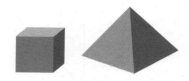

figura tridimensional Forma tridimensional: largo, ancho y alto.

---

trapezoid A four-sided plane shape with only two opposite sides that are the same length. (page 351)

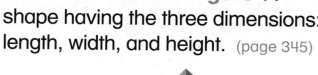

trapecio Figura de cuatro lados con sólo dos lados opuestos que tienen la misma longitud.

---

triangle A plane shape with three sides and three angles. (page 351)

triángulo Figura con tres lados y tres ángulos.

---

two-dimensional figure A shape such as a triangle or a square that is flat. (page 351)

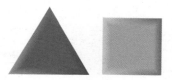

figura bidimensional Forma como un triángulo o un cuadrado plano.

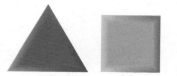

Glossary/Glosario

English		Español

U

unit fraction Any fraction with a numerator of 1. (page 283)

$$\frac{1}{2} \quad \frac{1}{3} \quad \frac{1}{4}$$

fracción unitaria Cualquier fracción cuyo numerador es 1.

$$\frac{1}{2} \quad \frac{1}{3} \quad \frac{1}{4}$$

V

vertex A point on a solid shape where two or more *edges* meet.

(page 347)

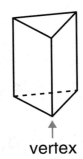

vertex

vértice Punto en una figura bidimensional o tridimensional donde se encuentran dos o más lados o aristas.

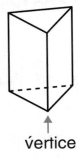

vértice

W

weight A measurement that tells how heavy an object is.

(page 421)

peso Medida que indica cuánto pesa un objeto.

whole The entire amount or object. (page 283)

el todo La cantidad total o el objeto completo.

Photo Credits

Photo Credits

Name _____

Count on 1, 2, and 3 (Use with Chapter 2)

1.
1	2	4	6	2	6
+ 0	+ 9	+ 3	+ 3	+ 6	+ 1

2.
9	2	4	3	3	1
+ 2	+ 5	+ 2	+ 5	+ 8	+ 3

3.
2	3	7	1	4	1
+ 2	+ 0	+ 1	+ 7	+ 1	+ 5

- ✂

Name _____

Count Back (Use with Chapter 3)

1.
2	6	4	7	5	8
− 1	− 2	− 2	− 3	− 1	− 2

2.
7	6	4	8	9	1
− 2	− 1	− 1	− 1	− 1	− 1

3.
9	3	9	2	5	6
− 3	− 3	− 2	− 2	− 3	− 3

Count on 1, 2, and 3 (Use with Chapter 2)

4.	6 + 2	5 + 1	2 + 7	2 + 4	7 + 3	9 + 3
5.	9 + 1	3 + 4	1 + 6	1 + 4	1 + 8	5 + 3
6.	8 + 2	1 + 9	7 + 2	3 + 7	3 + 6	8 + 1

- - - - - - - - - - - - - - - - -

Name _____

Count Back (Use with Chapter 3)

4.	3 − 1	7 − 3	3 − 3	4 − 3	8 − 1	9 − 3
5.	3 − 2	5 − 2	8 − 3	5 − 1	7 − 2	9 − 1
6.	6 − 2	7 − 1	6 − 1	8 − 3	9 − 2	5 − 3

Facts Practice

Name _____

Doubles and Near Doubles (Use with Chapter 4)

1.
$$\begin{array}{r} 5 \\ + 6 \\ \hline \end{array}$$
$$\begin{array}{r} 5 \\ + 4 \\ \hline \end{array}$$
$$\begin{array}{r} 4 \\ + 4 \\ \hline \end{array}$$
$$\begin{array}{r} 9 \\ + 9 \\ \hline \end{array}$$
$$\begin{array}{r} 6 \\ + 7 \\ \hline \end{array}$$
$$\begin{array}{r} 7 \\ + 8 \\ \hline \end{array}$$

2.
$$\begin{array}{r} 8 \\ + 8 \\ \hline \end{array}$$
$$\begin{array}{r} 8 \\ + 9 \\ \hline \end{array}$$
$$\begin{array}{r} 8 \\ + 7 \\ \hline \end{array}$$
$$\begin{array}{r} 6 \\ + 5 \\ \hline \end{array}$$
$$\begin{array}{r} 5 \\ + 5 \\ \hline \end{array}$$
$$\begin{array}{r} 7 \\ + 7 \\ \hline \end{array}$$

3.
$$\begin{array}{r} 4 \\ + 3 \\ \hline \end{array}$$
$$\begin{array}{r} 1 \\ + 2 \\ \hline \end{array}$$
$$\begin{array}{r} 4 \\ + 5 \\ \hline \end{array}$$
$$\begin{array}{r} 2 \\ + 2 \\ \hline \end{array}$$
$$\begin{array}{r} 7 \\ + 6 \\ \hline \end{array}$$
$$\begin{array}{r} 9 \\ + 8 \\ \hline \end{array}$$

- ✂

Name _____

Doubles (Use with Chapter 5)

1.
$$\begin{array}{r} 18 \\ - 9 \\ \hline \end{array}$$
$$\begin{array}{r} 2 \\ - 1 \\ \hline \end{array}$$
$$\begin{array}{r} 10 \\ - 5 \\ \hline \end{array}$$
$$\begin{array}{r} 6 \\ - 3 \\ \hline \end{array}$$
$$\begin{array}{r} 8 \\ - 4 \\ \hline \end{array}$$
$$\begin{array}{r} 12 \\ - 6 \\ \hline \end{array}$$

2.
$$\begin{array}{r} 14 \\ - 7 \\ \hline \end{array}$$
$$\begin{array}{r} 4 \\ - 2 \\ \hline \end{array}$$
$$\begin{array}{r} 12 \\ - 6 \\ \hline \end{array}$$
$$\begin{array}{r} 10 \\ - 5 \\ \hline \end{array}$$
$$\begin{array}{r} 14 \\ - 7 \\ \hline \end{array}$$
$$\begin{array}{r} 18 \\ - 9 \\ \hline \end{array}$$

3.
$$\begin{array}{r} 8 \\ - 4 \\ \hline \end{array}$$
$$\begin{array}{r} 16 \\ - 8 \\ \hline \end{array}$$
$$\begin{array}{r} 6 \\ - 3 \\ \hline \end{array}$$
$$\begin{array}{r} 4 \\ - 2 \\ \hline \end{array}$$
$$\begin{array}{r} 6 \\ - 3 \\ \hline \end{array}$$
$$\begin{array}{r} 16 \\ - 8 \\ \hline \end{array}$$

Name _____

Doubles and Near Doubles (Use with Chapter 4)

4.
$$\begin{array}{r} 2 \\ + 3 \\ \hline \end{array} \qquad \begin{array}{r} 8 \\ + 7 \\ \hline \end{array} \qquad \begin{array}{r} 7 \\ + 7 \\ \hline \end{array} \qquad \begin{array}{r} 4 \\ + 4 \\ \hline \end{array} \qquad \begin{array}{r} 4 \\ + 5 \\ \hline \end{array} \qquad \begin{array}{r} 4 \\ + 3 \\ \hline \end{array}$$

5.
$$\begin{array}{r} 1 \\ + 1 \\ \hline \end{array} \qquad \begin{array}{r} 5 \\ + 4 \\ \hline \end{array} \qquad \begin{array}{r} 0 \\ + 1 \\ \hline \end{array} \qquad \begin{array}{r} 0 \\ + 0 \\ \hline \end{array} \qquad \begin{array}{r} 6 \\ + 5 \\ \hline \end{array} \qquad \begin{array}{r} 1 \\ + 0 \\ \hline \end{array}$$

6.
$$\begin{array}{r} 6 \\ + 6 \\ \hline \end{array} \qquad \begin{array}{r} 2 \\ + 1 \\ \hline \end{array} \qquad \begin{array}{r} 5 \\ + 5 \\ \hline \end{array} \qquad \begin{array}{r} 3 \\ + 2 \\ \hline \end{array} \qquad \begin{array}{r} 3 \\ + 3 \\ \hline \end{array} \qquad \begin{array}{r} 2 \\ + 2 \\ \hline \end{array}$$

- -

Name _____

Doubles (Use with Chapter 5)

4.
$$\begin{array}{r} 12 \\ - 6 \\ \hline \end{array} \qquad \begin{array}{r} 14 \\ - 7 \\ \hline \end{array} \qquad \begin{array}{r} 18 \\ - 9 \\ \hline \end{array} \qquad \begin{array}{r} 8 \\ - 4 \\ \hline \end{array} \qquad \begin{array}{r} 2 \\ - 1 \\ \hline \end{array} \qquad \begin{array}{r} 16 \\ - 8 \\ \hline \end{array}$$

5.
$$\begin{array}{r} 4 \\ - 2 \\ \hline \end{array} \qquad \begin{array}{r} 10 \\ - 5 \\ \hline \end{array} \qquad \begin{array}{r} 12 \\ - 6 \\ \hline \end{array} \qquad \begin{array}{r} 10 \\ - 5 \\ \hline \end{array} \qquad \begin{array}{r} 18 \\ - 9 \\ \hline \end{array} \qquad \begin{array}{r} 14 \\ - 7 \\ \hline \end{array}$$

6.
$$\begin{array}{r} 16 \\ - 8 \\ \hline \end{array} \qquad \begin{array}{r} 6 \\ - 3 \\ \hline \end{array} \qquad \begin{array}{r} 4 \\ - 2 \\ \hline \end{array} \qquad \begin{array}{r} 6 \\ - 3 \\ \hline \end{array} \qquad \begin{array}{r} 8 \\ - 4 \\ \hline \end{array} \qquad \begin{array}{r} 2 \\ - 1 \\ \hline \end{array}$$

Name _____

Make a Ten (Use with Chapter 6)

1.
$$\begin{array}{r} 2 \\ + 8 \\ \hline \end{array}$$
$$\begin{array}{r} 6 \\ + 6 \\ \hline \end{array}$$
$$\begin{array}{r} 9 \\ + 6 \\ \hline \end{array}$$
$$\begin{array}{r} 3 \\ + 9 \\ \hline \end{array}$$
$$\begin{array}{r} 4 \\ + 6 \\ \hline \end{array}$$
$$\begin{array}{r} 5 \\ + 8 \\ \hline \end{array}$$

2.
$$\begin{array}{r} 6 \\ + 8 \\ \hline \end{array}$$
$$\begin{array}{r} 7 \\ + 7 \\ \hline \end{array}$$
$$\begin{array}{r} 7 \\ + 9 \\ \hline \end{array}$$
$$\begin{array}{r} 9 \\ + 5 \\ \hline \end{array}$$
$$\begin{array}{r} 5 \\ + 7 \\ \hline \end{array}$$
$$\begin{array}{r} 9 \\ + 9 \\ \hline \end{array}$$

3.
$$\begin{array}{r} 8 \\ + 8 \\ \hline \end{array}$$
$$\begin{array}{r} 6 \\ + 5 \\ \hline \end{array}$$
$$\begin{array}{r} 7 \\ + 4 \\ \hline \end{array}$$
$$\begin{array}{r} 8 \\ + 6 \\ \hline \end{array}$$
$$\begin{array}{r} 9 \\ + 7 \\ \hline \end{array}$$
$$\begin{array}{r} 7 \\ + 6 \\ \hline \end{array}$$

- ✂

Name _____

Facts to 10 (Use with Chapter 7)

1.
$$\begin{array}{r} 9 \\ + 1 \\ \hline \end{array}$$
$$\begin{array}{r} 4 \\ + 4 \\ \hline \end{array}$$
$$\begin{array}{r} 4 \\ + 6 \\ \hline \end{array}$$
$$\begin{array}{r} 6 \\ + 4 \\ \hline \end{array}$$
$$\begin{array}{r} 5 \\ + 1 \\ \hline \end{array}$$
$$\begin{array}{r} 2 \\ + 1 \\ \hline \end{array}$$

2.
$$\begin{array}{r} 4 \\ + 5 \\ \hline \end{array}$$
$$\begin{array}{r} 8 \\ + 2 \\ \hline \end{array}$$
$$\begin{array}{r} 5 \\ + 5 \\ \hline \end{array}$$
$$\begin{array}{r} 2 \\ + 3 \\ \hline \end{array}$$
$$\begin{array}{r} 2 \\ + 6 \\ \hline \end{array}$$
$$\begin{array}{r} 6 \\ + 2 \\ \hline \end{array}$$

3.
$$\begin{array}{r} 1 \\ + 6 \\ \hline \end{array}$$
$$\begin{array}{r} 5 \\ + 3 \\ \hline \end{array}$$
$$\begin{array}{r} 2 \\ + 7 \\ \hline \end{array}$$
$$\begin{array}{r} 3 \\ + 7 \\ \hline \end{array}$$
$$\begin{array}{r} 8 \\ + 0 \\ \hline \end{array}$$
$$\begin{array}{r} 7 \\ + 3 \\ \hline \end{array}$$

Make a Ten (Use with Chapter 6)

4.
$$7 + 3 \qquad 2 + 9 \qquad 4 + 8 \qquad 4 + 9 \qquad 9 + 8 \qquad 4 + 7$$

5.
$$6 + 4 \qquad 5 + 5 \qquad 6 + 7 \qquad 3 + 7 \qquad 9 + 3 \qquad 7 + 5$$

6.
$$3 + 8 \qquad 7 + 8 \qquad 5 + 6 \qquad 1 + 9 \qquad 6 + 9 \qquad 5 + 9$$

- -

Name _____

Facts to 10 (Use with Chapter 7)

4.
$$4 + 6 \qquad 1 + 7 \qquad 2 + 8 \qquad 1 + 9 \qquad 7 + 1 \qquad 0 + 8$$

5.
$$2 + 5 \qquad 4 + 2 \qquad 9 + 1 \qquad 6 + 0 \qquad 4 + 3 \qquad 3 + 6$$

6.
$$3 + 4 \qquad 1 + 8 \qquad 3 + 5 \qquad 7 + 2 \qquad 3 + 7 \qquad 4 + 1$$

Facts Practice

Name _____

Facts to 10 (Use with Chapter 8)

1.
$$\begin{array}{r} 9 \\ +1 \\ \hline \end{array}$$
$$\begin{array}{r} 4 \\ +4 \\ \hline \end{array}$$
$$\begin{array}{r} 4 \\ +6 \\ \hline \end{array}$$
$$\begin{array}{r} 6 \\ +4 \\ \hline \end{array}$$
$$\begin{array}{r} 5 \\ +1 \\ \hline \end{array}$$
$$\begin{array}{r} 2 \\ +1 \\ \hline \end{array}$$

2.
$$\begin{array}{r} 4 \\ +5 \\ \hline \end{array}$$
$$\begin{array}{r} 8 \\ +2 \\ \hline \end{array}$$
$$\begin{array}{r} 5 \\ +5 \\ \hline \end{array}$$
$$\begin{array}{r} 2 \\ +3 \\ \hline \end{array}$$
$$\begin{array}{r} 2 \\ +6 \\ \hline \end{array}$$
$$\begin{array}{r} 6 \\ +2 \\ \hline \end{array}$$

3.
$$\begin{array}{r} 1 \\ +6 \\ \hline \end{array}$$
$$\begin{array}{r} 5 \\ +3 \\ \hline \end{array}$$
$$\begin{array}{r} 2 \\ +7 \\ \hline \end{array}$$
$$\begin{array}{r} 3 \\ +7 \\ \hline \end{array}$$
$$\begin{array}{r} 8 \\ +0 \\ \hline \end{array}$$
$$\begin{array}{r} 7 \\ +3 \\ \hline \end{array}$$

Name _____

Facts to 12 (Use with Chapter 8)

1.
$$\begin{array}{r} 3 \\ +5 \\ \hline \end{array}$$
$$\begin{array}{r} 4 \\ +8 \\ \hline \end{array}$$
$$\begin{array}{r} 8 \\ +4 \\ \hline \end{array}$$
$$\begin{array}{r} 0 \\ +8 \\ \hline \end{array}$$
$$\begin{array}{r} 5 \\ +2 \\ \hline \end{array}$$
$$\begin{array}{r} 3 \\ +4 \\ \hline \end{array}$$

2.
$$\begin{array}{r} 6 \\ +5 \\ \hline \end{array}$$
$$\begin{array}{r} 2 \\ +5 \\ \hline \end{array}$$
$$\begin{array}{r} 4 \\ +2 \\ \hline \end{array}$$
$$\begin{array}{r} 9 \\ +1 \\ \hline \end{array}$$
$$\begin{array}{r} 5 \\ +6 \\ \hline \end{array}$$
$$\begin{array}{r} 7 \\ +4 \\ \hline \end{array}$$

3.
$$\begin{array}{r} 5 \\ +4 \\ \hline \end{array}$$
$$\begin{array}{r} 1 \\ +1 \\ \hline \end{array}$$
$$\begin{array}{r} 7 \\ +1 \\ \hline \end{array}$$
$$\begin{array}{r} 0 \\ +3 \\ \hline \end{array}$$
$$\begin{array}{r} 4 \\ +7 \\ \hline \end{array}$$
$$\begin{array}{r} 8 \\ +1 \\ \hline \end{array}$$

Name _____

Facts to 10 (Use with Chapter 8)

4. 4	1	2	1	7	0
+ 6	+ 7	+ 8	+ 9	+ 1	+ 8
5. 2	4	9	6	4	3
+ 5	+ 2	+ 1	+ 0	+ 3	+ 6
6. 3	1	3	7	3	4
+ 4	+ 8	+ 5	+ 2	+ 7	+ 1

- -

Name _____

Facts to 12 (Use with Chapter 8)

4. 7	4	3	8	2	5
+ 5	+ 3	+ 6	+ 3	+ 4	+ 7
5. 2	2	1	3	6	8
+ 6	+ 2	+ 5	+ 6	+ 6	+ 2
6. 5	6	2	1	9	3
+ 3	+ 1	+ 7	+ 7	+ 2	+ 3

Facts Practice

WorkMat I

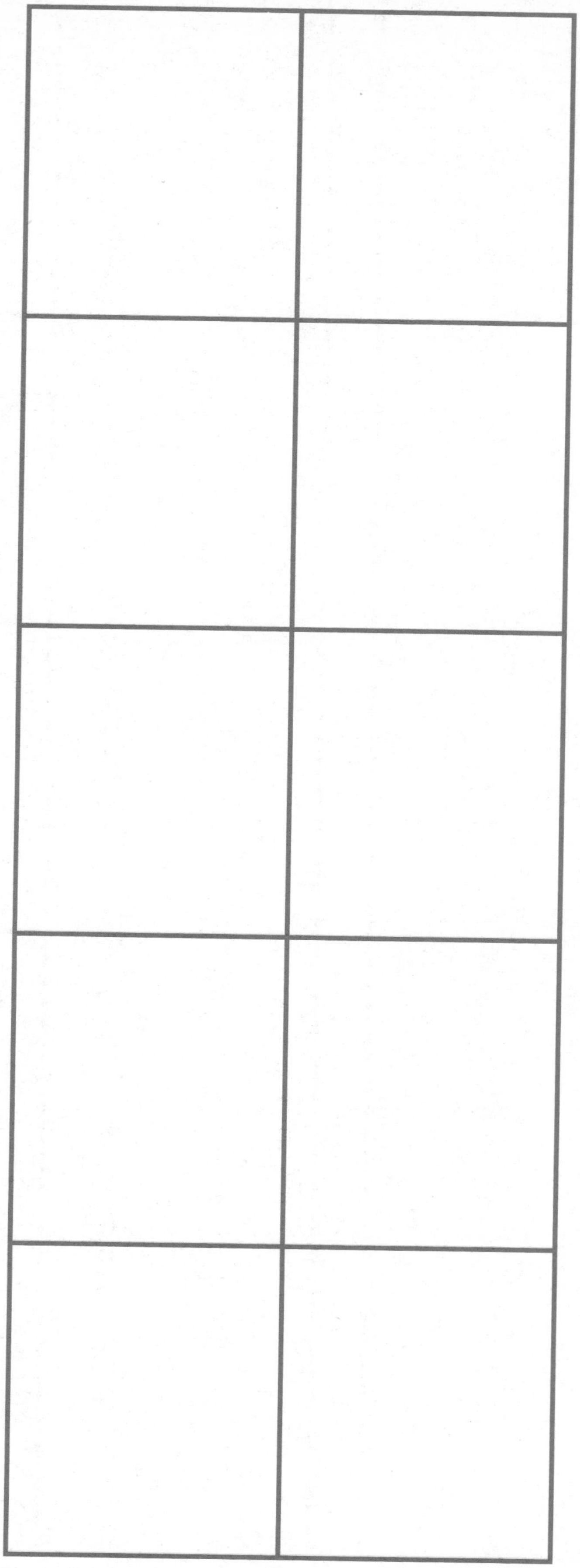

WorkMat I: Ten–Frame

WorkMat 2

WorkMat 2: Ten–Frame

WorkMat 3

Part

Part

Whole

0 1 2 3 4 5 6 7 8 9 10 11 12 13 14 15 16 17 18 19 20

21 22 23 24 25 26 27 28 29 30 31 32 33 34 35 36 37 38 39 40

41 42 43 44 45 46 47 48 49 50 51 52 53 54 55 56 57 58 59 60

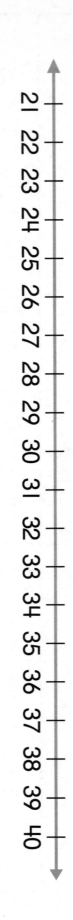

WorkMat 5

Tens	Ones

WorkMat 6: Tens and Ones Chart

WorkMat 7

Hundreds	Tens	Ones

WorkMat 7: Hundreds, Tens, and Ones Chart

Thousands	Hundreds	Tens	Ones

WorkMat 8: Thousands, Hundreds, Tens, and Ones Chart